Felted Tweed
Collection

by
Lisa Richardson

ROWAN

Gallery

Bessie

pattern. **p36** ≈ *image.* **p7**

Bertha

pattern. **p34** ≈ *image.* **p12**

Ethel

pattern. **p30** ≈ *image.* **p8**

Maude

pattern. **p39** ≈ *image.* **p15**

Pearl

pattern. **p26** ≈ *image.* **p11**

Hattie

pattern. **p28** ≈ *image.* **p17**

Rose

pattern. **p24** ≈ *image.* **p18**

ROWAN

Felted Tweed
Collection

by
Lisa Richardson

With distinctive colourwork
and delightful textures, this collection
by Lisa Richardson, emanates
style and comfort.

Felted Tweed
Collection

by
Lisa Richardson

Bessie

Felted Tweed
Collection

by
Lisa Richardson

Ethel

Felted Tweed
Collection

by
Lisa Richardson

Pearl

Felted Tweed
Collection

by
Lisa Richardson

Bertha

Felted Tweed
Collection

by
Lisa Richardson

_____

Maude

Felted Tweed
Collection

by
Lisa Richardson

_____

Hattie

Patterns

Felted Tweed
Collection

by
Lisa Richardson

Rose

Felted Tweed

a felted effect yarn made with merino wool & alpaca

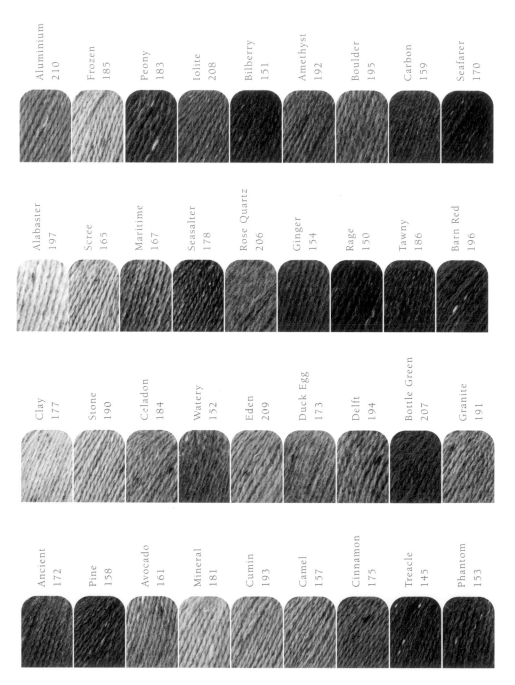

Row 1: Aluminium 210 · Frozen 185 · Peony 183 · Iolite 208 · Bilberry 151 · Amethyst 192 · Boulder 195 · Carbon 159 · Seafarer 170

Row 2: Alabaster 197 · Scree 165 · Maritime 167 · Seasalter 178 · Rose Quartz 206 · Ginger 154 · Rage 150 · Tawny 186 · Barn Red 196

Row 3: Clay 177 · Stone 190 · Celadon 184 · Watery 152 · Eden 209 · Duck Egg 173 · Delft 194 · Bottle Green 207 · Granite 191

Row 4: Ancient 172 · Pine 158 · Avocado 161 · Mineral 181 · Cumin 193 · Camel 157 · Cinnamon 175 · Treacle 145 · Phantom 153

Felted Tweed

Colours by Kaffe Fassett

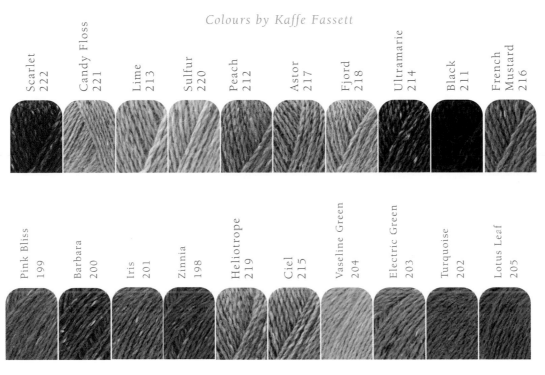

Scarlet 222 · Candy Floss 221 · Lime 213 · Sulfur 220 · Peach 212 · Astor 217 · Fjord 218 · Ultramarie 214 · Black 211 · French Mustard 216

Pink Bliss 199 · Barbara 200 · Iris 201 · Zinnia 198 · Heliotrope 219 · Ciel 215 · Vaseline Green 204 · Electric Green 203 · Turquoise 202 · Lotus Leaf 205

50% Wool 25% Alpaca 25% Viscose › approx 175m (191yds) per 50g ball

3¾ -4 mm | 9-8 UK | 5-6 US › 22-24 sts | 30-32 rows

Felted Tweed Colour
Arriving Autumn Winter

Felted Tweed Colour

by Kaffe Fassett

Succulent
027 NEW

Chestnut
024 NEW

Blush
021 NEW

Magenta
023 NEW

Chartreuse
028 NEW

Amethyst
026 NEW

Ripe
022 NEW

Frost
025 NEW

50% Wool 25% Alpaca 25% Viscose › approx 175m (191yds) per 50g ball

3¾ -4 mm | 9-8 UK | 5-6 US › 22-24 sts | 30-32 rows ›

Rose

Lisa Richardson

●●○○

SIZE

To fit bust

71-76	81-86	91-97	102-107	112-117	122-127	132-137	142-147	152-157	cm
28-30	32-34	36-38	40-42	44-46	48-50	52-54	56-58	60-62	in

Actual bust measurement of garment

101.5	111.5	121.5	131.5	141.5	151.5	161.5	171.5	183.5	cm
40	44	47¾	51¾	55¾	59¾	63½	67½	72¼	in

YARN

Felted Tweed

A Seasalter 178

4	5	5	6	6	7	7	8	8	x 50gm

B Cumin 193

3	3	4	4	4	5	5	5	6	x 50gm

NEEDLES

1 pair 3¼mm (no 10) (US 3) needles
1 pair 3¾mm (no 9) (US 5) needles
3¼mm (no 10) (US 3) circular needle at least 100 cm long

BUTTONS – 3 x 1.8 cm wooden buttons.

TENSION

24 sts and 32 rows to 10 cm measured over st st, using 3¾mm (US 5) needles.

BACK

Using 3¼mm (US 3) needles and yarn B cast on 122 [134: 146: 158: 170: 182: 194: 206: 220] sts.
Work in g st for 6 rows, ending with RS facing for next row.
Change to 3¾mm (US 5) needles.
Beg with a K row, now work in st st throughout as folls:
Work 72 [76: 76: 76: 78: 80: 80: 82: 82] rows straight, ending with RS facing for next row.
Break off yarn B and join in yarn A.
Work a further 74 [76: 82: 86: 90: 96: 98: 102: 104] rows straight, ending with RS facing for next row.

Shape shoulders

Cast off 4 [4: 5: 5: 6: 6: 7: 7: 7] sts at beg of next 10 [4: 10: 12: 12: 10: 12: 14: 8] rows, then - [5: -: -: -: 7: -: -: 8] sts at beg of next - [6: -: -: -: 2: -: -: 6] rows. 82 [88: 96: 98: 98: 108: 110: 108: 116] sts.

Shape back neck

Next row (RS): Cast off 4 [5: 6: 6: 6: 7: 7: 7: 8] sts, K until there are 19 [20: 23: 23: 23: 26: 27: 26: 29] sts on right needle and turn, leaving rem sts on a holder.
Work each side of neck separately:
Dec 1 st at neck edge of next 5 rows **and at same time** cast off 4 [5: 6: 6: 6: 7: 7: 7: 8] sts at beg of 2nd row and 5 [5: 6: 6: 6: 7: 7: 7: 8] sts at beg of foll alt row.
Cast off rem 5 [5: 6: 6: 6: 7: 8: 7: 8] sts.
With RS facing, slip centre 36 [38: 38: 40: 40: 42: 42: 42: 42] sts onto a holder (for band), rejoin yarn and K to end.
Complete to match first side, reversing shapings.

LEFT FRONT

Using 3¼mm (US 3) needles and yarn B cast on 59 [65: 71: 77: 83: 89: 95: 101: 108] sts.
Work in g st for 6 rows, ending with RS facing for next row.
Change to 3¾mm (US 5) needles.
Beg with a K row, now work in st st throughout as folls:
Work 72 [76: 76: 76: 78: 80: 80: 82: 82] rows straight, ending with RS facing for next row.
Break off yarn B and join in yarn A.

Shape front slope

Dec 1 st at end of next and 2 [3: 20: 21: 20: 20: 19: 17: 16] foll alt [alt: 4th: 4th: 4th: 4th: 4th: 4th: 4th] rows, then on 17 [17: -: -: 1: 2: 3: 5: 6] foll 4th [4th: -: -: 6th: 6th: 6th: 6th: 6th] rows.
39 [44: 50: 55: 61: 66: 72: 78: 85] sts.
Work 1 [1: 1: 1: 3: 3: 3: 3: 3] rows.

Shape shoulder

Cast off 4 [4: 5: 5: 6: 6: 7: 7: 7] sts at beg of next and foll 6 [1: 4: 5: 8: 4: 8: 9: 3] alt rows, then 5 [5: 6: 6: -: 7: -: -: 8] sts at beg of foll 1 [6: 3: 3: -: 4: -: -: 6] alt rows **and at same time** dec 1 st at neck edge of 3rd row.
Work 1 row.
Cast off rem 5 [5: 6: 6: 6: 7: 8: 7: 8] sts.

RIGHT FRONT

Using 3¼mm (US 3) needles and yarn B cast on 59 [65: 71: 77: 83: 89: 95: 101: 108] sts.
Work in g st for 6 rows, ending with RS facing for next row.
Change to 3¾mm (US 5) needles.
Beg with a K row, now work in st st throughout as folls:
Work 72 [76: 76: 76: 78: 80: 80: 82: 82] rows straight, ending with RS facing for next row.
Break off yarn B and join in yarn A.
Complete as given for left front, reversing shapings.

SLEEVES

Using 3¼mm (US 3) needles and yarn A cast on 67 [69: 71: 73: 73: 77: 77: 79: 79] sts.
Work in g st for 6 rows, ending with RS facing for next row.
Change to 3¾mm (US 5) needles.
Beg with a K row, now work in st st shaping sides by inc 1 st at each end of 9th [9th: 9th: 7th: 5th: 3rd: 3rd: 3rd: 3rd] and every foll 16th [14th: 10th: 8th: 6th: 6th:4th: 4th: 4th] row to 81 [83: 93: 101: 97: 115: 91: 107: 117] sts, then on every foll - [16th: -: -: 8th: -: 6th: 6th: 6th] row until there are - [85: -: -: 107: -: 119: 125: 129] sts.
Cont straight until sleeve meas 40 [41: 41: 42: 42: 42: 42: 42: 42] cm, ending with RS facing for next row.
Cast off.

MAKING UP

Press as described on the information page.
Join both shoulder seams using back stitch, or mattress stitch if preferred.

Front band

With RS facing and using 3¼mm (US 3) circular needle and yarn B, beg and ending at front cast-on edges, pick up and knit 53 [55: 57: 57: 57: 59: 59: 59: 59] sts up right front opening edge to beg of front slope shaping, 61 [63: 67: 71: 75: 78: 80: 83: 86] sts up right front slope, and 5 sts down right side of back neck, K across 36 [38: 38: 40: 40: 42: 42: 42: 42] sts on back holder, then pick up and knit 5 sts up left side of back neck, 61 [63: 67: 71: 75: 78: 80: 83: 86] sts down left front slope to beg of front slope shaping, and 53 [55: 57: 57: 57: 59: 59: 59: 59] sts down left front opening edge.
274 [284: 296: 306: 314: 326: 330: 336: 342] sts.
Work in g st for 6 rows, ending with **WS** facing for next row.
Row 7 (WS): K to last 52 [54: 56: 56: 56: 58: 58: 58: 58], ★K2tog, yfwd (to make a buttonhole), K20 [21: 22: 22: 22: 23: 23: 23: 23], rep from ★ once more, K2tog, yfwd (to make 3rd buttonhole), K to end.
Work in g st for a further 7 rows, ending with **WS** facing for next row.
Cast off knitwise (on **WS**).

Pockets (make 2, 1 in each colour)

Using 3¾mm (US 5) needles and yarn A or B cast on 34 sts.
Beg with a K row, work 42 rows in st st.
Change to 3¼mm (US 3) needles and work 9 rows in g st, ending with **WS** facing for next row.
Cast off knitwise (on **WS**).
Mark points along side seam edge 17.5[18.5: 20: 21.5: 23: 24.5: 25.5: 26.5: 27.5]cm either side of shoulder seams (to denote base of armhole openings). Sew patch pockets in position using photograph as a guide.
See information page for finishing instructions, setting in sleeves using the straight cast-off method.

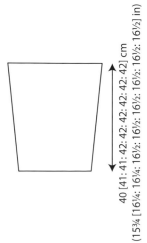

40 [41: 41: 42: 42: 42: 42: 42: 42] cm
(15¾ [16¼: 16¼: 16½: 16½: 16½: 16½: 16½: 16½] in)

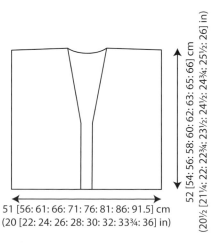

51 [56: 61: 66: 71: 76: 81: 86: 91.5] cm
(20 [22: 24: 26: 28: 30: 32: 33¾: 36] in)

52 [54: 56: 58: 60: 62: 63: 65: 66] cm
(20½ [21¼: 22: 22¾: 23½: 24½: 24¾: 25½: 26] in)

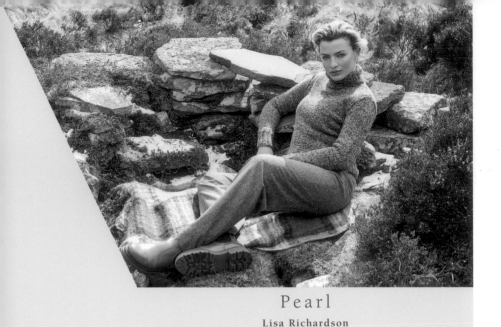

Pearl
Lisa Richardson
● ● ○ ○

SIZE
To fit bust

71-76	81-86	91-97	102-107	112-117	122-127	132-137	142-147	152-157	cm
28-30	32-34	36-38	40-42	44-46	48-50	52-54	56-58	60-62	in

Actual bust measurement of garment

84	94	104	114	124	134	144	154	164	cm
33	37	41	45	48¾	52¾	56½	60¾	64½	in

YARN
Felted Tweed

A Duck Egg 173

5	5	6	6	7	8	8	9	9	x 50gm

B Tawny 186

5	5	6	6	7	7	8	8	9	x 50gm

NEEDLES
1 pair 4½mm (no 7) (US 7) needles
1 pair 5mm (no 6) (US 8) needles

TENSION
16 sts and 23 rows to 10 cm measured over st st, using 5mm (US 8) needles and one strand each of yarns A and B held together.

BACK
Using 4½mm (US 7) needles and one strand each of yarns A and B held together cast on 66 [74: 82: 90: 98: 106: 114: 122: 130] sts.
Row 1 (RS): K2, *P2, K2, rep from * to end.
Row 2: P2, *K2, P2, rep from * to end.
These 2 rows form rib.
Cont in rib for a further 16 rows, inc 1 st in centre of last row and ending with RS facing for next row. 67 [75: 83: 91: 99: 107: 115: 123: 131] sts.
Change to 5mm (US 8) needles.
Beg with a K row, now work in st st throughout as folls:

Cont straight until back meas 32.5 [33.5: 34: 34: 35: 35.5: 35.5: 36.5: 36.5] cm, ending with RS facing for next row.
Shape armholes
Cast off 4 [5: 5: 5: 6: 6: 6: 7: 7] sts at beg of next 2 rows. 59 [65: 73: 81: 87: 95: 103: 109: 117] sts.
Next row (RS): K2, sl 1, K1, psso, K to last 4 sts, K2tog, K2.
Next row: P2, P2tog, P to last 4 sts, P2tog tbl, P2.
55 [61: 69: 77: 83: 91: 99: 105: 113] sts.
Working all decreases as set by last 2 rows, cont as folls:
Dec 1 st at each end of next 1 [1: 3: 5: 5: 7: 7: 9: 9] rows, then on foll 1 [2: 3: 3: 3: 3: 5: 5: 7] alt rows.
51 [55: 57: 61: 67: 71: 75: 77: 81] sts.
Cont straight until armhole meas 18 [19: 20.5: 22: 23.5: 25: 26: 27: 28] cm, ending with RS facing for next row.
Shape shoulders and back neck
Next row (RS): Cast off 4 [4: 5: 5: 6: 6: 7: 7: 8] sts, K until there are 12 [13: 13: 14: 16: 17: 18: 19: 20] sts on right needle and turn, leaving rem sts on a holder.
Work each side of neck separately:
Dec 1 st at neck edge of next 3 rows **and at same time** cast off 4 [5: 5: 5: 6: 7: 7: 8: 8] sts at beg of 2nd row.
Cast off rem 5 [5: 5: 6: 7: 7: 8: 8: 9] sts.
With RS facing, slip centre 19 [21: 21: 23: 23: 25: 25: 25: 25] sts onto another holder (for neckband), rejoin yarns and K to end.
Complete to match first side, reversing shapings.

FRONT
Work as given for back until 12 [12: 12: 14: 14: 16: 16: 16: 18] rows less have been worked than on back to beg of shoulders and back neck shaping, ending with RS facing for next row.
Shape front neck
Next row (RS): K19 [20: 21: 23: 26: 28: 30: 31: 34] and turn, leaving rem sts on a holder.
Work each side of neck separately.
Dec 1 st at neck edge of next 2 rows, then on foll 2 [2: 2: 3: 3: 4: 4: 4: 5] alt rows, then on foll 4th row.
14 [15: 16: 17: 20: 21: 23: 24: 26] sts.
Work 1 row.
Shape shoulder
Cast off 4 [4: 5: 5: 6: 6: 7: 7: 8] sts at beg of next row, then 4 [5: 5: 5: 6: 7: 7: 8: 8] sts at beg of foll alt row **and at same time** dec 1 st at neck edge of 3rd row.
Work 1 row.
Cast off rem 5 [5: 5: 6: 7: 7: 8: 8: 9] sts.
With RS facing, slip centre 13 [15: 15: 15: 15: 15: 15: 15: 13] sts onto another holder (for neckband), rejoin yarns and K to end.
Complete to match first side, reversing shapings.

SLEEVES
Using 4½mm (US 7) needles and one strand each of yarns A and B held together cast on 34 [38: 38: 42: 42: 42: 42: 46: 46] sts.
Work in rib as given for back for 22 rows, inc [dec: inc: dec: dec: inc: inc: dec: dec] 1 st in centre of last row and ending with RS facing for next row. 35 [37: 39: 41: 41: 43: 43: 45: 45] sts.
Change to 5mm (US 8) needles.
Beg with a K row, now work in st st shaping sides by inc 1 st at each end of 7th [7th: 7th: 5th: 5th: 5th: 3rd: 3rd: 3rd] and every foll 8th [8th: 8th: 6th: 6th: 6th: 4th: 4th: 4th] row to 45 [55: 57: 47: 63: 65: 53: 55: 67] sts, then on every foll 10th [-: -: 8th: 8th: 8th: 6th: 6th: 6th] row until there are 51 [-: -: 61: 65: 67: 71: 73: 77] sts.
Cont straight until sleeve meas 44 [45: 45: 46: 46: 46: 46: 46: 46] cm, ending with RS facing for next row.
Shape top
Cast off 4 [5: 5: 5: 6: 6: 6: 7: 7] sts at beg of next 2 rows. 43 [45: 47: 51: 53: 55: 59: 59: 63] sts.
Working all decreases as set on Back, cont as folls:

Dec 1 st at each end of next 3 rows, then on foll 2 alt rows, then on 3 [3: 4: 4: 4: 5: 4: 5: 4] foll 4th rows. 27 [29: 29: 33: 35: 35: 41: 39: 45] sts.

Work 1 row.

Dec 1 st at each end of next and every foll alt row until 23 sts rem, then on foll 5 rows, ending with RS facing for next row.

Cast off 3 sts at beg of next 2 rows.

Cast off rem 7 sts.

MAKING UP

Press as described on the information page.

Join right shoulder seam using back stitch, or mattress st if preferred.

Collar

With RS facing, using 4½mm (US 7) needles and one strand each of yarns A and B held together pick up and knit 15 [15: 15: 17: 17: 19: 19: 19: 20] sts down left side of front neck, K across 13 [15: 15: 15: 15: 15: 15: 15: 13] sts on front holder inc 2 [2: 2: 3: 3: 2: 2: 2: 2] sts evenly, pick up and knit 15 [15: 15: 17: 17: 19: 19: 19: 20] sts up right side of front neck, and 4 sts down right side of back neck, K across 19 [21: 21: 23: 23: 25: 25: 25: 25] sts on back holder inc 2 [2: 2: 3: 3: 2: 2: 2: 2] sts evenly, then pick up and knit 4 sts up left side of back neck. 74 [78: 78: 86: 86: 90: 90: 90: 90] sts.

Beg with row 1, work in rib as given for back until collar meas 8cm, from pick-up row.

Change to 5mm (US 8) needles.

Cont in rib until collar meas 19 cm from pick-up row, ending with **WS** of body (RS of collar) facing for next row.

Cast off loosely in rib.

See information page for finishing instructions, setting in sleeves using the set-in method and reversing collar seam for last 10cm (for turn-back).

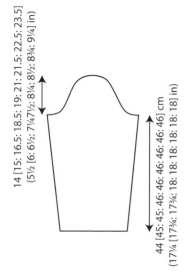

14 [15: 16.5: 18.5: 19: 21: 21.5: 22.5: 23.5]
(5½ [6: 6½: 7¼:7½: 8¼: 8½: 8¾: 9¼] in)

44 [45: 45: 46: 46: 46: 46: 46: 46] cm
(17¼ [17¾: 17¾: 18: 18: 18: 18: 18: 18] in)

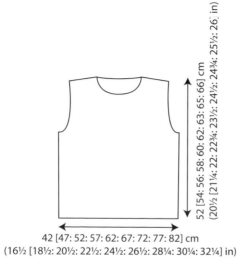

52 [54: 56: 58: 60: 62: 63: 65: 66] cm
(20½ [21¼: 22: 22¾: 23½: 24½: 24¾: 25½: 26] in)

42 [47: 52: 57: 62: 67: 72: 77: 82] cm
(16½ [18½: 20½: 22½: 24½: 26½: 28¼: 30¼: 32¼] in)

Hattie

Lisa Richardson

●●○○

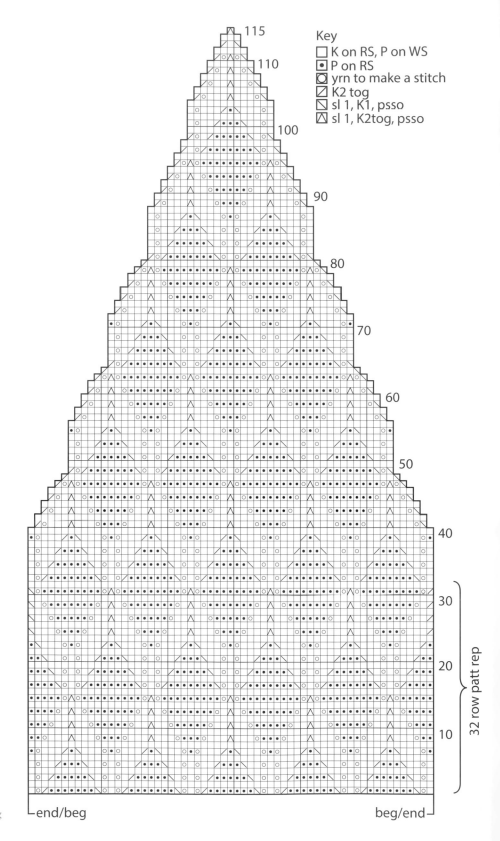

Key
□ K on RS, P on WS
• P on RS
○ yrn to make a stitch
▨ K2 tog
◩ sl 1, K1, psso
▲ sl 1, K2tog, psso

YARN
Felted Tweed
4   x 50gm
(photographed in Seasalter 178)

NEEDLES
1 pair 4mm (no 8) (US 6) needles

TENSION
22 sts and 33 rows to 10 cm measured over patt, using 4mm (US 6) needles.

FINISHED SIZE
Completed scarf is approx. 28 cm (11 in) wide and 187 cm (73½ in) long.

SCARF
First section
Using 4mm (US 6) needles and waste yarn cast on 61 sts.
Beg with a K row, work in st-st for 2 rows, ending with RS facing for next row.
Break off waste yarn and join in working yarn.
Beg and ending rows as indicated, cont in patt from chart as folls:
Rep rows 1 to 32, 7 times, then rows 33 to 40 once, ending with RS facing for next row.
Shape point
Working rows 41 -115 of chart, cont in patt as folls:
Dec 1 st at each end of next and 3 foll alt rows. 53 sts.
Dec 1 st at each end of next 2 rows. 49 sts.
Work 7 rows straight, ending with RS facing for next row.
Rep last 16 rows twice more. 25 sts.
Dec 1 st at each end of next and 5 foll alt rows. 13 sts.
Work 5 rows straight, ending with RS facing for next row.
Dec 1 st at each end of next and 5 foll alt rows. 1 st.
Fasten off.
Second section
Unravel the waste yarn from the first section and slip these 61 sts onto a needle. With RS facing, using

4mm (US 6) needles, beg and ending rows as indicated, cont in patt from chart as folls:
Work rows 31 and 32 once, rep rows 1 to 32, 7 times, then rows 33 to 40 once, ending with RS facing for next row.

Shape point
Working rows 41 –115 of chart, cont in patt as folls:
Dec 1 st at each end of next and 3 foll alt rows. 53 sts.
Dec 1 st at each end of next 2 rows. 49 sts.
Work 7 rows straight, ending with RS facing for next row.
Rep last 16 rows twice more. 25 sts.
Dec 1 st at each end of next and 5 foll alt rows. 13 sts.
Work 5 rows straight, ending with RS facing for next row.
Dec 1 st at each end of next and 5 foll alt rows. 1 st.
Fasten off.

MAKING UP
Press as described on the information page.

Ethel
Lisa Richardson

SIZE
To fit bust

71-76	81-86	91-97	102-107	112-117	122-127	132-137	142-147	152-157	cm
28-30	32-34	36-38	40-42	44-46	48-50	52-54	56-58	60-62	in

Actual bust measurement of garment

105.5	116	125.5	136	145.5	156	165.5	176	185.5	cm
41½	45¾	49½	53½	57¼	61½	65¼	69¼	73	in

YARN
Felted Tweed

A Bilberry 151

3	3	4	4	4	4	5	5	5	x 50gm

B Avocado 161

2	2	2	2	2	2	2	2	2	x 50gm

C Ginger 154

1	2	2	2	2	2	2	2	2	x 50gm

D Treacle 145

2	3	3	3	3	3	4	4	4	x 50gm

E Bottle Green 207

2	2	2	2	2	2	2	2	2	x 50gm

F Rose Quartz 206

3	3	3	3	3	4	4	4	4	x 50gm

NEEDLES
1 pair 3¼mm (no 10) (US 3) needles
1 pair 3¾mm (no 9) (US 5) needles
3¼mm (no 10) (US 3) circular needle at least 180 cm long

BUTTONS – 5 x 1.8 cm buttons.

TENSION
26 sts and 27 rows to 10 cm measured over patterned st st, using 3¾mm (US 5) needles.

BACK
Using 3¼mm (US 3) needles and yarn A cast on 139 [151: 163: 175: 187: 201: 213: 227: 239] sts.
Row 1 (RS): P0 [0: 0: 0: 0: 0: 0: 1: 1], K2 [2: 2: 2: 2: 2: 3: 3: 3], *P3, K3, rep from * to last 5 [5: 5: 5: 5: 0: 0: 1: 1] sts, P3 [3: 3: 3: 3: 0: 0: 1: 1], K2 [2: 2: 2: 2: 0: 0: 0: 0].
Row 2: P2 [2: 2: 2: 2: 0: 0: 0: 0], K3 [3: 3: 3: 3: 0: 0: 1: 1], * P3, K3, rep from * to last 2 [2: 2: 2: 2: 3: 3: 4: 4] sts, P2 [2: 2: 2: 2: 3: 3: 3: 3], K0 [0: 0: 0: 0: 0: 0: 1: 1].
These 2 rows form rib.
Cont in rib for a further 20 rows, dec [-: -: inc: inc: inc: inc: inc: inc] 2 [: : 2: 2: 2: 2: 2: 2] sts evenly across last row and ending with RS facing for next row.
137 [151: 163: 177: 189: 203: 215: 229: 241] sts.
Change to 3¾mm (US 5) needles.
Beg and ending rows as indicated, using the **fairisle** technique as described on the information page, repeating the 22 st patt rep 5 [5: 7: 7: 7: 9: 9: 9: 9] times across each row, and the 88 row patt repeat throughout, which is worked entirely in st st beg with a K row, cont in patt from body chart as folls:
Cont straight until back meas 77 [79: 81: 83: 85: 87: 88: 90: 91] cm, ending with RS facing for next row.

Shape shoulders and back neck
Next row (RS): Cast off 11 [12: 14: 15: 17: 18: 20: 22: 23] sts, patt until there are 39 [44: 48: 53: 57: 62: 66: 71: 76] sts on right needle and turn, leaving rem sts on a holder.
Work each side of neck separately:
Dec 1 st at neck edge of next 5 rows **and at same time** cast off 11 [13: 14: 16: 17: 19: 20: 22: 23] sts at beg of 2nd row, then 11 [13: 14: 16: 17: 19: 20: 22: 24] sts at beg of foll alt row.
Cast off rem 12 [13: 15: 16: 18: 19: 21: 22: 24] sts.
With RS facing, slip centre 37 [39: 39: 41: 41: 43: 43: 43: 43] sts onto a holder (for band), rejoin appropriate yarns and patt to end.
Complete to match first side, reversing shapings.

POCKET LININGS (make 2)
Using 3¾mm (US 5) needles and yarn D cast on 29 [33: 33: 33: 35: 35: 35: 35: 35] sts.
Beg with a K row, work 33 [39: 39: 39: 43: 43: 43: 43: 43] rows in st-st, ending with **WS** facing for next row.
Next row (WS): P4 [4: 4: 4: 5: 5: 5: 5: 5], M1, (P4 [5: 5: 5: 5: 5: 5: 5: 5], M1) 5 times, P5 [4: 4: 4: 5: 5: 5: 5: 5].
35 [39: 39: 39: 41: 41: 41: 41: 41] sts.
Break yarn and leave sts on a holder.

LEFT FRONT
Using 3¼mm (US 3) needles and yarn A cast on 69 [75: 81: 87: 93: 100: 106: 113: 119] sts.
Row 1 (RS): P0 [0: 0: 0: 0: 0: 0: 1: 1], K2 [2: 2: 2: 2: 3: 3: 3: 3], *P3, K3, rep from * to last st, K1.
Row 2: K1, * P3, K3, rep from * to last 2 [2: 2: 2: 2: 3: 3: 4: 4] sts, P2 [2: 2: 2: 2: 3: 3: 3: 3], K0 [0: 0: 0: 0: 0: 0: 1: 1].
These 2 rows form rib.
Cont in rib for a further 20 rows, dec 3 [2: 2: 2: 1: 1: 1: 1: 1] sts evenly across last row and ending with RS facing for next row. 66 [73: 79: 86: 92: 99: 105: 112: 118] sts.
Change to 3¾mm (US 5) needles.
Beg and ending rows as indicated, repeating the 22 st patt rep 2 [2: 3: 3: 3: 4: 4: 4: 4] times across each row, and the 88 row patt repeat throughout, which is worked entirely in st st beg with a K row, cont in patt from body chart as folls:
Cont straight for 32 [36: 36: 36: 38: 38: 38: 38: 38] rows, ending with RS facing for next row.

Place pocket
Keeping patt correct, cont as folls:
Next row (RS): Patt 8 [9: 15: 20: 24: 29: 35: 42: 48] sts, slip next 35 [39: 39: 39: 41: 41: 41: 41: 41] sts onto a holder (for pocket top) and, in their place patt across 35 [39: 39: 39: 41: 41: 41: 41: 41] sts of first pocket lining, patt rem 23 [25: 25: 27: 27: 29: 29: 29: 29] sts.
Working pocket sts into patt to replace these on holder, cont straight until 70 [72: 76: 80: 84: 88: 92: 94: 96] rows less have been worked than on back to beg of shoulder shaping, ending with RS facing for next row.

Shape front slope

Keeping patt correct, dec 1 st at end of next and foll 7 [8: 6: 6: 4: 4: 2: 1: 0] alt rows, then on 13 [13: 15: 16: 18: 19: 21: 22: 23] foll 4th rows. 45 [51: 57: 63: 69: 75: 81: 88: 94] sts.

Work 3 rows.

Shape shoulder

Cast off 11 [12: 14: 15: 17: 18: 20: 22: 23] sts at beg of next and foll 2 [–: 2 –: 2: –: 2: 2: 1] alt rows, then – [13: –: 16: –: 19: –: –: 24] sts at beg of foll – [2: –: 2: –: 2: –: –: 1] alt rows.

Work 1 row.

Cast off rem 12 [13: 15: 16: 18: 19: 21: 22: 24] sts.

RIGHT FRONT

Using 3¼mm (US 3) needles and yarn A cast on 69 [75: 81: 87: 93: 100: 106: 113: 119] sts.

Row 1 (RS): K4, *P3, K3, rep from * to last 5 [5: 5: 5: 5: 0: 0: 1: 1] sts, P3 [3: 3: 3: 3: 0: 0: 1: 1], K2 [2: 2: 2: 2: 0: 0: 0: 0].

Row 2: P2 [2: 2: 2: 2: 0: 0: 0: 0], K3 [3: 3: 3: 3: 0: 0: 1: 1], * P3, K3, rep from * to last 4 sts, P3, K1.

These 2 rows form rib.

Cont in rib for a further 20 rows, dec 3 [2: 2: 1: 1: 1: 1: 1: 1] sts evenly across last row and ending with RS facing for next row. 66 [73: 79: 86: 92: 99: 105: 112: 118] sts.

Change to 3¾mm (US 5) needles.

Beg and ending rows as indicated, repeating the 22 st patt rep 2 [2: 3: 3: 3: 4: 4: 4: 4] times across each row, and the 88 row patt repeat throughout, which is worked entirely in st st beg with a K row, cont in patt from body chart as folls:

Cont straight for 32 [36: 36: 36: 38: 38: 38: 38: 38] rows, ending with RS facing for next row.

Place pocket

Keeping patt correct, cont as folls:

Next row (RS): Patt 23 [25: 25: 27: 27: 29: 29: 29: 29] sts, slip next 35 [39: 39: 39: 41: 41: 41: 41: 41] sts onto a holder (for pocket top) and, in their place patt across 35 [39: 39: 39: 41: 41: 41: 41: 41] sts of second pocket lining, patt rem 8 [9: 15: 20: 24: 29: 35: 42: 48] sts.

Complete as given for left front, reversing shapings.

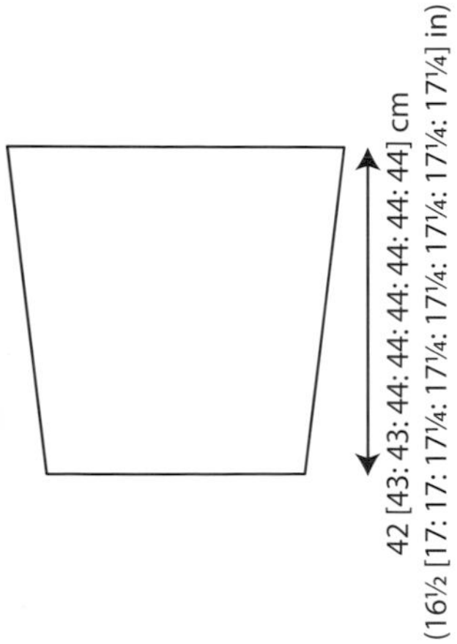

42 [43: 43: 44: 44: 44: 44: 44: 44] cm
(16½ [17: 17: 17¼: 17¼: 17¼: 17¼: 17¼: 17¼] in)

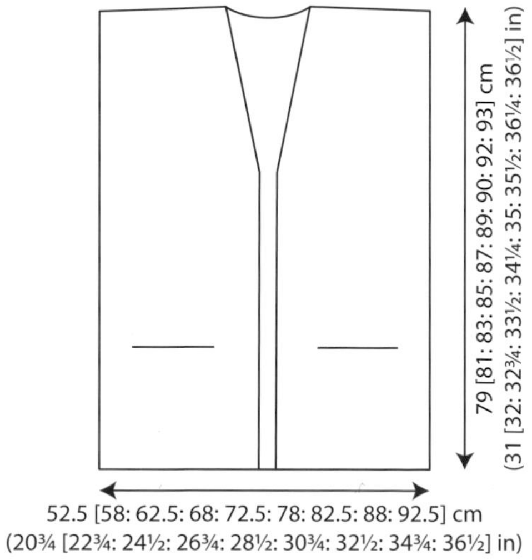

79 [81: 83: 85: 87: 89: 90: 92: 93] cm
(31 [32: 32¾: 33½: 34¼: 35: 35½: 36¼: 36½] in)
52.5 [58: 62.5: 68: 72.5: 78: 82.5: 88: 92.5] cm
(20¾ [22¾: 24½: 26¾: 28½: 30¾: 32½: 34¾: 36½] in)

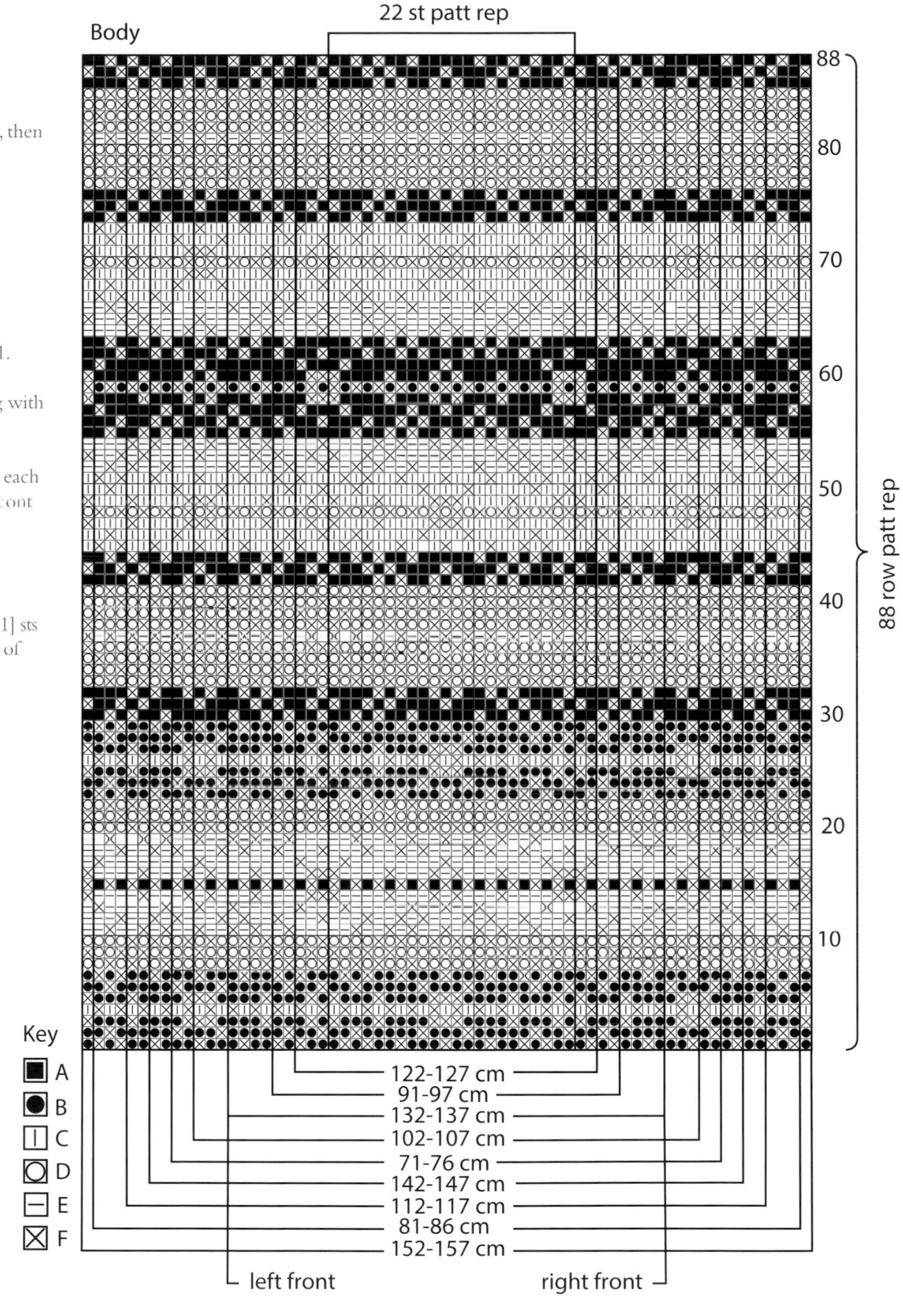

Body
22 st patt rep
88
80
70
60
50
40
30
20
10
88 row patt rep
122-127 cm
91-97 cm
132-137 cm
102-107 cm
71-76 cm
142-147 cm
112-117 cm
81-86 cm
152-157 cm
left front
right front
Key
■ A
● B
| C
○ D
— E
☒ F

SLEEVES

Using 3¼mm (US 3) needles and yarn A cast on 73 [79: 79: 79: 79: 87: 87: 89: 89] sts.

Work in rib as given for back for 22 rows, inc [dec: –: inc: inc: –: –: –: –] 2 [2: –: 4: 4: –: –: –: –] sts evenly across last row and ending with RS facing for next row. 75 [77: 79: 83: 83: 87: 87: 89: 89] sts.

Change to 3¾mm (US 5) needles.

Beg and ending rows as indicated, using the **fairisle** technique as described on the information page, repeating the 22 st patt 3 times across each row, and the 88 row patt repeat throughout, which is worked entirely in st st beg with a K row, cont in patt from sleeve chart as folls:

(**Note:** Increases are **NOT** shown on the chart.) Inc 1 st at each end of 3rd and every foll 4th [4th: 2nd: 2nd: 2nd: 2nd: 2nd: 2nd: 2nd] row to 95 [107: 85: 93: 105: 117: 129: 135: 147] sts, then on every foll 6th [6th: 4th: 4th: 4th: 4th: 4th: 4th: 4th] row until there are 109 [115: 123: 131: 137: 145: 151: 155: 161] sts, taking inc sts into patt.

Cont straight until sleeve meas 42 [43: 43: 44: 44: 44: 44: 44: 44] cm, ending with RS facing for next row.

Cast off.

MAKING UP

Press as described on the information page.

Join both shoulder seams using back stitch, or mattress stitch if preferred.

Front band

With RS facing and using 3¼mm (US 3) circular needle and yarn A, beg and ending at front cast-on edges, pick up and knit 127 [130: 130: 131: 131: 135: 135: 137: 137] sts up right front opening edge to beg of front slope shaping, 70 [72: 75: 79: 82: 86: 89: 93: 96] sts up right front slope, and 6 sts down right side of back neck, K across 37 [39: 39: 41: 41: 43: 43: 43: 43] sts on back holder, then pick up and knit 6 sts up left side of back neck, 70 [72: 75: 79: 82: 86: 89: 93: 96] sts down left front slope to beg of front slope shaping, and 127 [130: 130: 131: 131: 135: 135: 137: 137] sts down left front opening edge. 443 [455: 461: 473: 479: 497: 503: 515: 521] sts.

Row 1 (WS): K1, *P3, K3, rep from * to last 4 sts, P3, K1.

Row 2: K4, *P3, K3, rep from * to last st, K1.

These 2 rows form rib.

Work a further 2 rows in rib, ending with **WS** facing for next row.

Row 5 (WS): Rib to last 126 [129: 129: 130: 130: 134: 134: 135: 135] sts, *rib2tog, yrn (to make a buttonhole), rib 27 [28: 28: 28: 28: 29: 29: 29: 29], rep from * 3 times more, rib2tog, yrn (to make 5th buttonhole), rib to end.

Work in rib for a further 4 rows, ending with RS facing for next row.

Cast off in rib.

Pocket tops (both alike)

Slip 35 [39: 39: 39: 41: 41: 41: 41: 41] sts on pocket top holder onto 3¼mm (US 3) needles and rejoin yarn D with RS facing.

K 1 row, inc 1 [1: 1: 1: 3: 3: 3: 3: 3] sts evenly. 36 [40: 40: 40: 44: 44: 44: 44: 44] sts.

Row 1 (WS): P1, *K2, P2, rep from * to last 3 sts, K2, P1.

Row 2: K1, *P2, K2, rep from * to last 3 sts, P2, K1.

Rep last 2 rows 3 times more, ending with **WS** facing for next row.

Cast off in rib.

Mark points along side seam edge 22 [23: 24.5: 26: 27: 29: 30: 30.5: 32] cm either side of shoulder seams (to denote base of armhole openings).

See information page for finishing instructions, setting in sleeves using the straight cast-off method.

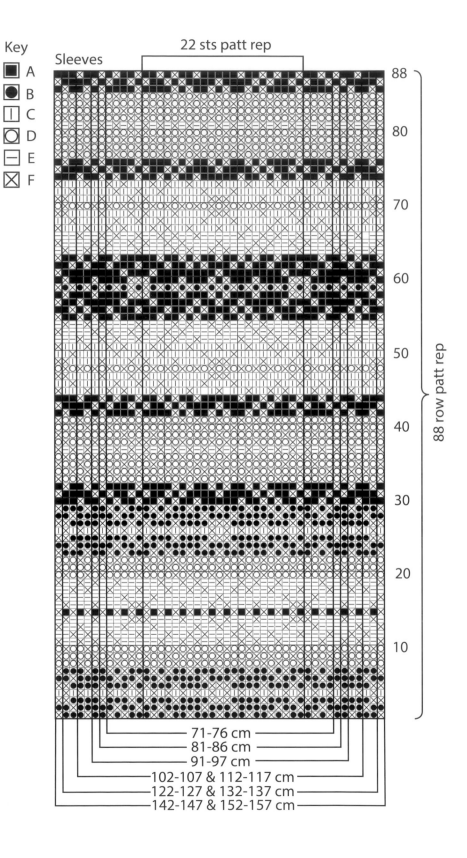

Key
■ A
● B
▯ C
◯ D
⊟ E
⊠ F

Sleeves

22 sts patt rep

88 row patt rep

88
80
70
60
50
40
30
20
10

71-76 cm
81-86 cm
91-97 cm
102-107 & 112-117 cm
122-127 & 132-137 cm
142-147 & 152-157 cm

Bertha

Lisa Richardson

● ● ● ○

SIZE

To fit bust

71-76	81-86	91-97	102-107	112-117	122-127	132-137	142-147	152-157	cm
28-30	32-34	36-38	40-42	44-46	48-50	52-54	56-58	60-62	in

Actual bust measurement of garment

86	95.5	106	115.5	126	135.5	146	155.5	166	cm
33¾	37½	41¾	45½	49½	53¼	57½	61¼	65¼	in

YARN

Felted Tweed

A Stone 190

4	4	5	5	6	6	7	7	8	x 50gm

B Ginger 154

1	1	1	1	1	1	1	1	1	x 50gm

C Bilberry 151

1	1	1	1	1	1	1	1	1	x 50gm

D Watery 152

1	1	1	1	1	1	1	1	1	x 50gm

E Tawny 186

1	1	1	1	1	1	1	1	1	x 50gm

F Avocado 161

1	1	1	1	1	1	1	1	1	x 50gm

NEEDLES

1 pair 3¼mm (no 10) (US 3) needles
1 pair 3¾mm (no 9) (US 5) needles
3¼mm (no 10) (US 3) circular needle at least 100cm long

TENSION

26 sts and 27 rows to 10 cm measured over patterned st st, using 3¾mm (US 5) needles.

BACK

Using 3¼mm (US 3) needles and yarn A cast on 114 [126: 138: 150: 166: 178: 190: 202: 218] sts.
Row 1 (RS): K2, *P2, K2, rep from * to end.
Row 2: P2, *K2, P2, rep from * to end.
These 2 rows form rib.
Cont in rib for a further 6 rows, ending with RS facing for next row.
Join in yarn E.
Using yarn E, work a further 2 rows in rib.
Break off yarn E.
Using yarn A, work a further 8 rows in rib, inc 0 [0: 2: 2: 0: 0: 2: 2: 0] sts evenly across last row and ending with RS facing for next row. 114 [126: 140: 152: 166: 178: 192: 204: 218] sts.
Change to 3¾mm (US 5) needles.
Next row (RS): Using A, K to end.
Beg and ending rows as indicated, using the **fairisle** technique as described on the information page repeating the 10 st patt rep 10 [11: 14: 14: 15: 16: 19: 19: 20] times across each row and repeating the 60 row patt rep throughout, now work in patt from chart, which is worked entirely in st st beg with a P row as folls:
Note: shaping is not shown on chart.
Keeping patt correct, dec 1 st at each end of 4th and 2 [3: 1: 2: 4: 1: 1: 4: 4] foll 14th [14th: 16th: 16th: 16th: 18th: 18th: 18th: 18th] rows, then on 2 [1: 3: 2: –: 3: 3: –: –] foll 12th [12th: 14th: 14th: –: 16th: 16th: –: –] rows. 104 [116: 130: 142: 156: 168: 182: 194: 208] sts. **★★**
Work 7 rows straight, ending with RS facing for next row.
Inc 1 st at each end of next and 3 [3: 1: 1: 3: 3: 3: 3: 3] foll 6th [6th: 4th: 4th: 4th: 4th: 4th: 4th: 4th] rows, then on – [–: 2: 2: –: –: –: –: –] foll – [–: 6th: 6th: –: –: –: –: –] rows, taking inc sts into patt. 112 [124: 138: 150: 164: 176: 190: 202: 216] sts.
Work 7 rows, ending with RS facing for next row. (Back should meas approx. 38.5 [39: 40: 40.5: 40.5: 41.5: 41.5: 43.5: 43.5] cm).
Place markers at both ends of last row to denote base of armhole openings.
Cont straight until back meas 27 [28: 29.5: 31: 32.5: 34: 35: 35: 36] cm **from markers**, ending with RS facing for next row.
Shape shoulders and back neck
Next row (RS): Cast off 7 [8: 10: 11: 13: 14: 16: 18: 19] sts, patt until there are 28 [32: 37: 41: 46: 50: 55: 59: 65] sts on right needle and turn, leaving rem sts on a holder.
Work each side of neck separately:
Dec 1 st at neck edge of next 5 rows **and at same time** cast off 7 [9: 10: 12: 13: 15: 16: 18: 20] sts at beg of 2nd row and foll 0 [1: 0: 1: 0: 1: 0: 1: 1] alt rows, then 8 [–: 11: –: 14: –: 17: –: –] sts at beg of foll 1 [–: 1: –: 1: –: 1: –: –] alt row.
Cast off rem 8 [9: 11: 12: 14: 15: 17: 18: 20] sts.
With RS facing, slip centre 42 [44: 44: 46: 46: 48: 48: 48: 48] sts onto a holder (for neckband), rejoin appropriate yarns and patt to end.
Complete to match first side, reversing shapings.

FRONT

Note: Do not start a contrast yarn patt motif at **centre front** within 6 rows of beg of front neck. If the division for front neck would be during a contrast yarn motif, work the sts at centre front in yarn A.
Work as given for Back to **★★**, ending with **WS** facing for next row.
Work 3 [3: 1: 1: 1: 1: 1: 1: 1] rows straight, ending with RS facing for next row.
Divide for front neck
Next row (RS): Patt 50 [56: 63: 69: 76: 82: 89: 95: 102], K2tog, and turn, leaving rem sts on a holder.
51 [57: 64: 70: 77: 83: 90: 96: 103] sts.
Work each side of neck separately.
Taking inc sts into patt, inc 1 st at beg of 4th [4th: 6th: 6th: 6th: 6th: 6th: 6th: 6th] and 3 [3: 1: 1: 3: 3: 3: 3: 3] foll 6th [6th: 4th: 4th: 4th: 4th: 4th: 4th: 4th] rows, then on 0 [0: 2: 2: 0: 0: 0: 0: 0] foll 6th rows **and at same time** dec 1 st at neck edge on 2nd and foll 3 [4: 3: 3: 3: 2: 1: 1: 0] alt rows, then on 3 [3: 3: 3: 2: 3: 3: 3: 4] foll 4th rows.
48 [53: 61: 67: 75: 81: 89: 95: 102] sts.

Dec 1 st at neck edge of 2nd [4th: 2nd: 2nd: 2nd: 4th: 2nd: 2nd: 4th] and 1 [0: 1: 1: 1: 0: 1: 1: 0] foll 4th rows. 46 [52: 59: 65: 73: 80: 87: 93: 101] sts.
Work 1 [3: 1: 1: 1: 3: 1: 1: 3] rows straight, ending with RS facing for next row.
Place markers at both ends of last row to denote base of armhole openings.
Dec 1 st at neck edge on 3rd [next: 3rd: 3rd: 3rd: next: 3rd: 3rd: next] and 15 [16: 16: 17: 18: 20: 20: 20: 21] foll 4th rows. 30 [35: 42: 47: 54: 59: 66: 72: 79] sts.
Cont straight until front matches back to beg of shoulder shaping, ending with RS facing for next row.

Shape shoulder
Cast off 7 [8: 10: 11: 13: 14: 16: 18: 19] sts at beg of next and foll 1 [0: 1: 0: 1: 0: 1: 2: 0] alt rows, then 8 [9: 11: 12: 14: 15: 17: –: 20] sts at beg of foll 1 [2: 1: 2: 1: 2: 1: –: 2] alt rows.
Work 1 row.
Cast off rem 8 [9: 11: 12: 14: 15: 17: 18: 20] sts.
With RS facing, rejoin appropriate yarns and K2tog, patt to end. 51 [57: 64: 70: 77: 83: 90: 96: 103] sts.
Complete to match first side, reversing shapings.

MAKING UP
Press as described on the information page.
Join right shoulder seam using back stitch, or mattress st if preferred.

Neckband
With RS facing, using 3¼mm (US 3) circular needle and yarn A, pick up and knit 96 [96: 100: 104: 108: 112: 116: 116: 116] sts down left side of front neck, pick up loop at centre of V and knit into back of this loop (mark this st with a coloured thread), pick up and knit 96 [96: 100: 104: 108: 112: 116: 116: 116] sts up right side of front neck, and 6 sts down right side of back neck, K across 42 [44: 44: 46: 46: 48: 48: 48: 48] sts on back holder inc 2 [–: –: 2: 2: –: –: –: –] sts evenly, then pick up and knit 6 sts up left side of back neck. 249 [249: 257: 269: 277: 285: 293: 293: 293] sts.
Row 1 (WS): *P2, K2, rep from * to marked st, P marked st, ** K2, P2, rep from ** to end.
This row sets position of rib.
Keeping rib correct as set, cont as folls:
Row 2: Rib to within 1 st of marked st, slip 2 sts as though to K2tog (marked st is 2nd of these 2 sts), K1, pass 2 slipped sts over, rib to end.
Row 3: Rib to marked st, P marked st, rib to end.
Rep last 2 rows twice more, ending with RS facing for next row.
243 [243: 251: 263: 271: 279: 287: 287: 287] sts.
Join in yarn E, and rep rows 2 and 3 once more. 241 [241: 249: 261: 269: 277: 285: 285: 285] sts.
Break off yarn E.
Using yarn A, rep rows 2 and 3, 3 times more. 235 [235: 243: 255: 263: 271: 279: 279: 279] sts.
Cast off in rib, still decreasing either side of marked st as before.
Join left shoulder and neckband seam.

Armhole borders (both alike)
With RS facing, using 3¼mm (US 3) needles and yarn A, pick up and knit 134 [138: 146: 154: 162: 166: 174: 174: 178] sts evenly along armhole opening edge between marked points.
Beg with row 2, work in rib as given for back for 3 rows, ending with RS facing for next row.
Keeping rib correct as now set, cont as folls:
Row 4 (RS): Rib 124 [128: 136: 144: 152: 156: 164: 164: 168] sts, wrap next st (by slipping next st from left needle onto right needle, taking yarn to opposite side of work between needles and then slipping same st back onto left needle)
Row 5: Rib 114 [118: 126: 134: 142: 146: 154: 154: 158] sts, wrap next st and turn.
Row 6: Rib 108 [112: 120: 128: 136: 140: 148: 148: 152] sts, wrap next st and turn.
Row 7: Rib 102 [106: 114: 122: 130: 134: 142: 142: 146] sts, wrap next st and turn.
Cont in this way, working 6 sts less sts every row as before, wrapping next st and turning, until the foll row has been worked.
Row 11 (WS): Rib 78 [82: 90: 98: 106: 110: 118: 118: 122] sts, wrap next st and turn.
Row 12: Rib to end.
Work 1 row across all sts, ending with RS facing for next row.
Cast off in rib.
See information page for finishing instructions.

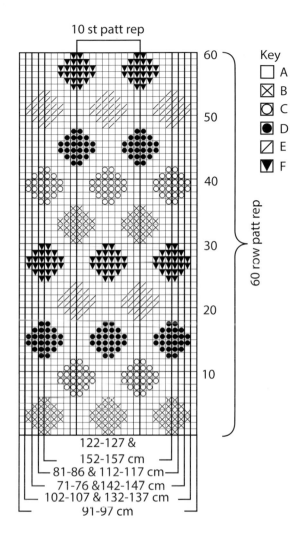

10 st patt rep

60 row patt rep

Key
A
B
C
D
E
F

122-127 &
152-157 cm
81-86 & 112-117 cm
71-76 &142-147 cm
102-107 & 132-137 cm
91-97 cm

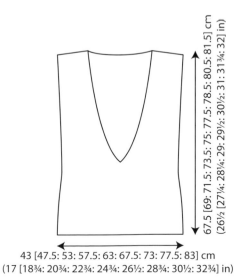

67.5 [69: 71.5: 73.5: 75: 77.5: 78.5: 80.5: 81.5] cm
(26½ [27¼: 28¼: 29: 29½: 30½: 31: 31¾: 32] in)

43 [47.5: 53: 57.5: 63: 67.5: 73: 77.5: 83] cm
(17 [18¾: 20¾: 22¾: 24¾: 26½: 28¾: 30½: 32¾] in)

BESSIE

Lisa Richardson

●●●○

SIZE

To fit bust

71-76	81-86	91-97	102-107	112-117	122-127	132-137	142-147	152-157	cm
28-30	32-34	36-38	40-42	44-46	48-50	52-54	56-58	60-62	in

Actual bust measurement of garment

110	119	130	139	150	159	170	179	190	cm
43¼	46¾	51¼	54¾	59	62½	67	70½	74¾	in

YARN

Felted Tweed

A Aluminium 210

2	3	3	3	3	4	4	4	4	x 50gm

B Avocado 161

3	3	3	3	3	4	4	4	4	x 50gm

C Tawny 186

2	2	2	2	3	3	3	3	3	x 50gm

D Zinnia 198

2	2	3	3	3	3	3	4	4	x 50gm

E Bottle Green 207

2	2	2	2	3	3	3	3	3	x 50gm

NEEDLES

1 pair 3¼mm (no 10) (US 3) needles
1 pair 3¾mm (no 9) (US 5) needles

TENSION

26 sts and 27 rows to 10 cm measured over patterned st st, using 3¾mm (US 5) needles.

BACK

Using 3¼mm (US 3) needles and yarn D cast on 145 [157: 169: 181: 193: 205: 223: 235: 247] sts.
Row 1 (RS): K2, *P3, K3, rep from * to last 5 sts, P3, K2.
Row 2: P2, *K3, P3, rep from * to last 5 sts, K3, P2.
These 2 rows form rib.

Cont in rib for a further 4 rows, ending with RS facing for next row.
Break off yarn D, join in yarn A.
Using yarn A, work a further 22 rows in rib, dec [dec: –: –: inc: inc: dec: dec: –] 2 [2: 2: –: –: 2: 2: 2: 2: –] sts evenly across last row and ending with RS facing for next row.
143 [155: 169: 181: 195: 207: 221: 233: 247] sts.
Change to 3¾mm (US 5) needles.
Beg and ending rows as indicated, using the **fairisle** technique as described on the information page, repeating the 24 st patt rep 5 [6: 7: 7: 8: 8: 9: 9: 10] times across each row, and the 32 row patt repeat throughout, which is worked entirely in st st beg with a K row, cont in patt from body chart as folls:
Work first 32 rows using colours from first rep, next 32 rows using colours from second rep, next 32 rows using colours from third rep, next 32 rows using colours from fourth rep.
These 128 rows form the full pattern and colour repeat, and are repeated.
Cont straight until back meas 63 [65: 67: 69: 71: 73: 74: 76: 77] cm, ending with RS facing for next row.
Shape shoulders and back neck
Next row (RS): Cast off 9 [11: 12: 14: 15: 17: 18: 20: 22] sts, patt until there are 35 [38: 44: 47: 53: 56: 62: 66: 71] sts on right needle and turn, leaving rem sts on a holder.
Work each side of neck separately:
Dec 1 st at neck edge of next 5 rows **and at same time** cast off 10 [11: 13: 14: 16: 17: 19: 20: 22] sts at beg of 2nd row and foll alt row.
Cast off rem 10 [11: 13: 14: 16: 17: 19: 21: 22] sts.
With RS facing, slip centre 55 [57: 57: 59: 59: 61: 61: 61: 61] sts onto a holder (for neckband), rejoin appropriate yarns and patt to end.
Complete to match first side, reversing shapings.

FRONT
Work as given for back until 24 [24: 24: 26: 26: 28: 28: 28: 28] rows less have been worked than on back to beg of back neck shaping, ending with RS facing for next row.
Shape front neck
Next row (RS): Patt 51 [56: 63: 69: 76: 82: 89: 95: 102] and turn, leaving rem sts on a holder.
Work each side of neck separately.
Dec 1 st at neck edge of next 4 rows, then on foll 5 [5: 5: 6: 6: 7: 7: 7: 7] alt rows, then on 2 foll 4th rows. 40 [45: 52: 57: 64: 69: 76: 82: 89] sts.
Work 1 row.
Shape shoulder
Cast off 9 [11: 12: 14: 15: 17: 18: 20: 22] sts at beg of next and foll – [2: –: 2: –: 2: –: 2: 2] alt rows, then 10 [–: 13: –: 16: –: 19: –: –] sts at beg of foll 2 [–: 2: –: 2: –: 2: –: –] alt row **and at same time** dec 1 st at neck edge of 3rd row.
Work 1 row.
Cast off rem 10 [11: 13: 14: 16: 17: 19: 21: 22] sts.
With RS facing, slip centre 41 [43: 43: 43: 43: 43: 43: 43: 43] sts onto another holder (for neckband), rejoin appropriate yarns and K to end.
Complete to match first side, reversing shapings.

SLEEVES
Using 3¼mm (US 3) needles and yarn C cast on 73 [79: 79: 79: 79: 85: 85: 85: 85] sts.
Work in rib as given for back for 6 rows, ending with RS facing for next row.
Break off yarn C, join in yarn B.
Using yarn B, cont in rib until sleeve meas 9 cm, inc [dec: –: inc: inc: inc: inc: inc: inc] 2 [2: –: 4: 4: 2: 2: 4: 4] sts evenly across last row and ending with RS facing for next row.
75 [77: 79: 83: 83: 87: 87: 89: 89] sts.
Change to 3¾mm (US 5) needles.
Beg and ending rows as indicated, using the **fairisle** technique as described on the information page, repeating the 24 st patt 3 times across each row, and the 32 row patt repeat throughout, which is worked entirely in st st beg with a K row, cont in patt from sleeve chart as folls:
(**Note:** Increases are **NOT** shown on the chart.) Work first 32 rows using colours from first rep as folls: Inc 1 st at each end of 3rd and every foll 6th [6th: 4th: 4th: 2nd: 2nd: 2nd: 2nd: 2nd] row to

85 [87: 95: 99: 91: 103: 111: 119: 119] sts, then on every foll – [–: –: –: 4th: 4th: 4th: –: –] row until there are – [–: –: –: 101: 109: 113: –: –] sts, taking inc sts into patt.

Work 5 [5: 1: 1: 3: 3: 3: 1: 1] rows straight to complete the 32 row patt.

Work the next 32 rows using colours from second rep as folls: Inc 1 st at each end of next [next: 5th: 3rd: next: next: next: next: next] and every foll 6th [6th: 6th: 4th: 4th: 4th:4th: 4th: 2nd] row to 93 [99: 105: 109: 117: 125: 129: 135: 133] sts, then on every foll 8th [–: –: 6th: –: –: –: –: 4th] row until there are 95 [–: –: 113: –: –: –: –: 141] sts, taking inc sts into patt.

Work 5 [1: 3: 1: 3: 3: 3: 3: 3] rows straight to complete the 32 row patt.

Work the next 11 [15: 15: 17: 17: 17: 17: 17: 17] rows using colours from third rep as folls: Inc 1 st at each end of 3rd [7th: 3rd: 5th: next: next: next: next: next] and every foll 8th [8th: 6th: 6th: 4th: 4th: 4th: 4th: 4th] row to 99 [103: 111: 119: 127: 135: 139: 145: 151] sts, taking inc sts into patt.

Work a further 13 rows straight, ending with row 24 [28: 28: 30: 30: 30: 30: 30: 30] of third rep and with RS facing for next row.

Cast off.

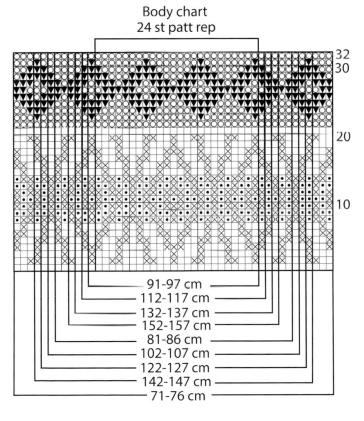

Body chart
24 st patt rep

91-97 cm
112-117 cm
132-137 cm
152-157 cm
81-86 cm
102-107 cm
122-127 cm
142-147 cm
71-76 cm

Key	1st rep	2nd rep	3rd rep	4th rep
☐	A	B	D	E
⊠	B	D	E	A
⊙	C	A	B	D
○	D	E	C	C
▼	E	C	A	B

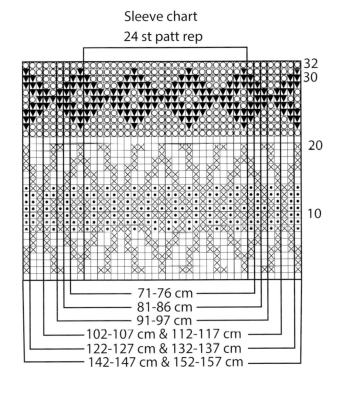

Sleeve chart
24 st patt rep

71-76 cm
81-86 cm
91-97 cm
102-107 cm & 112-117 cm
122-127 cm & 132-137 cm
142-147 cm & 152-157 cm

Key	1st rep	2nd rep	3rd rep
▼	A	B	E
•	B	D	C
○	C	E	D
☐	D	C	A
⊠	E	A	B

MAKING UP

Press as described on the information page.

Join right shoulder seam using back stitch, or mattress st if preferred.

Neckband

With RS facing, using 3¼mm (US 3) needles and yarn A, pick up and knit 26 [27: 27: 29: 29: 31: 31: 31: 33] sts down left side of front neck, K across 41 [43: 43: 43: 43: 43: 43: 43: 43] sts on front holder, pick up and knit 26 [27: 27: 29: 29: 31: 31: 31: 33] sts up right side of front neck, and 5 sts down right side of back neck, K across 55 [57: 57: 59: 59: 61: 61: 61: 61] sts on back holder, dec [dec: dec: dec: dec: dec: dec: dec: inc] 1 st at centre, then pick up and knit 5 sts up left side of back neck. 157 [163: 163: 169: 169: 175: 175: 175: 181] sts.

Row 1 (WS): P2, *K3, P3, rep from * to last 5 sts, K3, P2.

Row 2: K2, *P3, K3, rep from * to last 5 sts, P3, K2.

These 2 rows form rib.

Cont in rib for a further 3 rows, ending with RS facing for next row.

Next row: K2, *P2tog, P1, K3, rep from * to last 5 sts, P2tog, P1, K2. 131 [136: 136: 141: 141: 146: 146: 146: 151] sts.

Next row: P2, *K2, P3, rep from * to last 4 sts, K2, P2.

Next row: K2, *P2, K3, rep from * to last 4 sts, P2, K2.

Last 2 rows now set rib.

Cont in rib as now set for a further 3 rows.

Next row: K2, *P2tog, K3, rep from * to last 4 sts, P2tog, K2. 105 [109: 109: 113: 113: 117: 117: 117: 121] sts.

Next row: P2, *K1, P3, rep from * to last 3 sts, K1, P2.

Next row: K2, *P1, K3, rep from * to last 3 sts, P1, K2.

Last 2 rows now set rib.

Cont in rib as now set for a further 3 rows, ending with RS facing for next row.

Cast off in rib.

Join left shoulder and neckband seam.

Mark points along side seam edges 20 [20.5: 22: 24: 25.5: 27: 27.5: 29: 30] cm, either side of shoulder seams (to denote base of armhole openings.)

See information page for finishing instructions, setting in sleeves using the straight cast-off method.

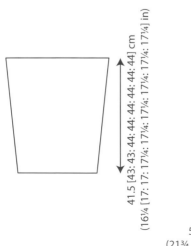

41.5 [43: 43: 44: 44: 44: 44: 44: 44] cm
(16¼ [17: 17: 17¼: 17¼: 17¼: 17¼: 17¼: 17¼] in)

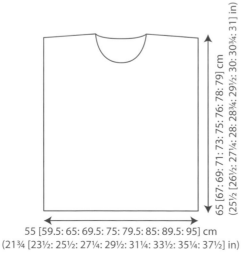

65 [67: 69: 71: 73: 75: 76: 78: 79] cm
(25½ [26½: 27¼: 28: 28¾: 29½: 30: 30¾: 31] in)

55 [59.5: 65: 69.5: 75: 79.5: 85: 89.5: 95] cm
(21¾ [23½: 25½: 27¼: 29½: 31¼: 33½: 35¼: 37½] in)

Maude

Lisa Richardson

● ● ○ ○

SIZE

To fit bust

71-76	81-86	91-97	102-107	112-117	122-127	132-137	142-147	152-157	cm
28-30	32-34	36-38	40-42	44-46	48-50	52-54	56-58	60-62	in

Actual bust measurement of garment

84	93.5	105	114.5	124	133.5	143	154.5	164	cm
33	36¾	41¼	45	48¾	52½	56¼	60¾	64½	in

YARN

Felted Tweed

7	8	9	9	10	11	12	12	13	x 50gm

(photographed in Tawny 186)

NEEDLES

1 pair 3¼mm (no 10) (US 3) needles
1 pair 4mm (no 8) (US 6) needles
3¼mm (no 10) (US 3) circular needle at least 120cm long
4.00mm (no 8) (US G6) crochet hook

TENSION

21 sts and 30 rows to 10 cm measured over patt using 4mm (US 6) needles.

SPECIAL ABBREVIATION

'make a ladder st' = slip 2 sts between markers off needle, and unravel to first row of pattern above g st (or as far as the stitch will unravel) to form dropped stitches. Insert 4.00mm (US G6) crochet hook into both of the dropped sts, hook three 'bars' above these stitches with the crochet hook, pull all three bars through the two stitches onto the hook to form a chain stitch. Cont to work a chain stitch using three 'bars' to top of work, slip st back onto left needle. (**Note:** work three bars where possible, ess bars can be worked at the end nearest the needle.)

BACK

Using 3¼mm (US 3) needles cast on 88 [98: 110: 120: 130: 140: 150: 162: 172] sts.
Work in g st for 8 rows, ending with RS facing for next row.

Change to 4mm (US 6) needles.
Now work in patt as folls:
Row 1 (RS): K4 [9: 2: 7: 12: 4: 9: 2: 7], ★ place marker on needle, K2, place another marker on needle, K11, rep from ★ to last 6 [11: 4: 9: 14: 6: 11: 4: 9] sts, place marker on needle, K2, place another marker on needle, K4 [9: 2: 7: 12: 4: 9: 2: 7].
Markers identify '2 ladder stitches'.
Row 2: P4 [9: 2: 7: 12: 4: 9: 2: 7], ★ slip marker onto right needle, P2, slip marker onto right needle, P11, rep from ★ to last 6 [11: 4: 9: 14: 6: 11: 4: 9] sts, slip marker onto right needle, P2, slip marker onto right needle, P4 [9: 2: 7: 12: 4: 9: 2: 7].
These 2 rows form patt, slipping markers onto right needle on every row.
Cont in patt until back meas 19 [20: 21: 22: 23: 25: 25.5: 26.5: 27] cm, ending with RS facing for next row.

Work belt casing

Next Row (RS): Patt 28 [33: 39: 44: 49: 54: 59: 65: 70] sts, slip next 32 sts onto a holder and leave at front of work, pick up and knit 32 sts from behind sts left on holder, patt rem 28 [33: 39: 44: 49: 54: 59: 65: 70] sts.
Work 17 rows in patt across all sts, ending with RS facing for next row.
Leave aside but do not break off yarn.
For casing section, slip 32 sts on holder onto 4mm (US 6) needles and rejoin a new ball of yarn with RS facing.
Next row (RS): K2, place a marker on needle, K2, place another marker on needle, (K11, place a marker on needle, K2, place another marker on needle) twice, K2.
Next row: K2, patt to last 2 sts, K2.
Rep last 2 rows 8 times more, slipping markers onto right needle on every row, ending with RS facing for next row.
Break yarn.
Return to 88 [98: 110: 120: 130: 140: 150: 162: 172] sts of main section, with RS facing and using original ball of yarn cont as folls:
Next row (RS): Patt first 28 [33: 39: 44: 49: 54: 59: 65: 70] sts of back section, then holding **WS** of casing section against RS of main section, K tog first st of casing section with next st of back section, (K tog next st of casing section with next st of back section) 31 times (to end of casing), patt rem 28 [33: 39: 44: 49: 54: 59: 65: 70] sts.
88 [98: 110: 120: 130: 140: 150: 162: 172] sts.
Cont in patt across all sts until back meas 43 [44: 44.5: 45: 45.5: 46: 46: 47: 47] cm, ending with RS facing for next row.

Shape raglan armhole

When working shaping you will need to make ladder sts as explained in the special abbreviation section. When casting off over the 'ladder stitches' do so as folls:
Sizes 71-76, 91-97, 122-127, 142-147 and 152-157cm only
Next row (RS): Cast off 3 [-: 1: -: -: 3: -: 1: 6] sts (one st on right needle), remove marker, 'make a ladder st', cast off 1 [-: 3: -: -: 3: -: 6: 1] sts, patt to last 6 [-: 4: -: -: 6: -: 4: 9] sts, remove marker, 'make a ladder st', remove marker, K4 [-: 2: -: -: 4: -: 2: 7].
Next row: Cast off 4 [-: 4: -: -: 6: -: 7: 7] sts, patt to end. 78 [-: 100: -: -: 126: -: 146: 156] sts.
Sizes 81-86, 102-107, 112-117 and 132-137cm only
Cast off - [5: -: 6: 6: -: 8: -: -] sts at beg of next 2 rows. - [88: -: 108: 118: -: 134: -: -] sts.
All sizes
(**Note:** When losing a stitch between markers due to working the ladder at the raglan shaping, do not decrease for the raglan on that row. Instead work K3 at raglan edges of the RS row. Stitch counts are not given after each row when decreases are made. Please refer to the stitch count after shaping is complete for the final figure.)
Keeping patt correct, cont as folls:
Next row (RS): K2, sl 1, K1, psso, patt to last 4 sts, K2tog, K2.
Next row: P2, P2tog, patt to last 4 sts, P2tog tbl, P2.
Working all decreases as set by last 2 rows (except on ladder rows – see note above), dec 1 st at each end of next 5 [11: 17: 19: 27: 27: 31: 41: 47] rows, then on foll 19 [17: 17: 18: 15: 18: 18: 14: 13] alt rows. 26 [28: 28: 30: 30: 32: 32: 32: 32] sts.
Work 1 row, ending with RS facing for next row.

Cast off rem sts, working ladders on rem ladder sts.

LEFT FRONT

Using 3¼mm (US 3) needles and cast on 53 [58: 64: 69: 74: 79: 84: 90: 95] sts.
Work in g st for 8 rows, ending with RS facing for next row.
Change to 4mm (US 6) needles.
Now work in patt as folls:
Row 1 (RS): K4 [9: 2: 7: 12: 4: 9: 2: 7], ★ place marker on needle, K2, place another marker on needle, K11, rep from ★ to last 10 sts, place marker on needle, K2, place another marker on needle, K8.
Markers identify '2 ladder stitches'.
Row 2: P8, ★ slip marker onto right needle, P2, slip marker onto right needle, P11, rep from ★ to last 6 [11: 4: 9: 14: 6: 11: 4: 9] sts, slip marker onto right needle, P2, slip marker onto right needle, P4 [9: 2: 7: 12: 4: 9: 2: 7].
These 2 rows form patt, slipping markers on every row.
Cont straight until 38 rows less have been worked than on back to beg of raglan armhole shaping, ending with RS facing for next row.
Shape front slope
(**Note:** When working shaping you will need to make ladder sts as explained in the special abbreviation section. When working the ladder st at the front slope shaping, do not decrease for the front slope on that row. Instead work K2 at front slope edge of the RS row. Stitch counts are not given after each row when decreases are made. Please refer to the stitch count after shaping is complete for the final figure)
Keeping patt correct, cont as folls:
Next row (RS): Patt to last 3 sts, K2tog, K1 (see note above).
Working front slope decreases as set by last row (except for ladder rows – see pattern note), dec 1 st at end of 4th and 8 foll 4th rows.
Work 1 row.
Shape raglan armhole
When working shaping you will need to make ladder sts as explained in the special abbreviation section. When casting off over the 'ladder stitches' do so as folls:
Sizes 71-76, 91-97, 122-127, 142-147 and 152-157cm only
Next row (RS): Cast off 3 [-: 1: -: -: 3: -: 1: 6] sts (one st on right needle), remove marker, 'make a ladder st', cast off 1 [-: 3: -: -: 3: -: 6: 1] sts, patt to last 2 sts, K2.
Sizes 81-86, 102-107, 112-117 and 132-137cm only
Next row (RS): Cast off - [5: -: 6: 6: -: 8: -: -] sts at beg of next row.
All sizes
Work 1 row.
(**Note:** When losing a stitch between markers due to working the ladder at the raglan shaping, do not decrease for the raglan on that row. Instead work K3 at raglan edge of the RS row. Stitch counts are not given after each row when decreases are made. Please refer to the stitch count after shaping is complete for the final figure.)
Working all raglan armhole decreases as set by back (see note above), dec 1 st at raglan armhole edge on next 7 [13: 19: 21: 29: 29: 33: 43: 49] rows, then on foll 17 [15: 15: 16: 13: 16: 16: 12: 11] alt rows, **and at same time** dec 1 st at front slope edge on next and 6 [8: 5: 6: 5: 5: 3: 2: -] foll 4th rows, then on 2 [1: 4: 4: 5: 6: 8: 9: 11] foll 6th rows. 5 sts.
Work 1 row.
Working any remaining ladders as required, **at same time** dec 1 st at raglan armhole edge on next and foll alt row.
Work 1 row, ending with RS facing for next row.
Next row (RS): Work rem sts together and fasten off.

RIGHT FRONT

Using 3¼mm (US 3) needles and cast on 53 [58: 64: 69: 74: 79: 84: 90: 95] sts.
Work in g st for 8 rows, ending with RS facing for next row.
Change to 4mm (US 6) needles.

Now work in patt as folls:
Row 1 (RS): K8, ★ place marker on needle, K2, place another marker on needle, K11, rep from ★ to last 6 [11: 4: 9: 14: 6: 11: 4: 9] sts, place marker on needle, K2, place another marker on needle, K4 [9: 2: 7: 12: 4: 9: 2: 7].
Markers identify '2 ladder stitches'.
Row 2: P4 [9: 2: 7: 12: 4: 9: 2: 7], ★ slip marker onto right needle, P2, slip marker onto right needle, P11, rep from ★ to last 10 sts, slip marker onto right needle, P2, slip marker onto right needle, P8.
These 2 rows form patt, slipping markers on every row.
Cont straight until 38 rows less have been worked than on back to beg of raglan armhole shaping, ending with RS facing for next row.
Shape front slope
(**Note:** When working shaping you will need to make ladder sts as explained in the special abbreviation section. When working the ladder st at the front slope shaping, do not decrease for the front slope on that row. Instead work K2 at front slope edge of the RS row. Stitch counts are not given after each row when decreases are made. Please refer to the stitch count after shaping is complete for the final figure) Keeping patt correct, cont as folls:
Next row (RS): K1, sl 1, K1, psso (see note above), patt to end.
Complete to match left front, reversing shapings.

SLEEVES

Using 3¼mm (US 3) needles and cast on 58 [62: 62: 66: 66: 66: 66: 70: 70] sts.
Row 1 (RS): K2, ★P2, K2, rep from ★ to end.
Row 2: P2, ★K2, P2, rep from ★ to end.
These 2 rows form rib.
Work in rib for a further 26 rows, dec 4 [4: 1: 3: 3: 2: 2: 3: 3] sts evenly across last row and ending with RS facing for next row. 54 [58: 61: 63: 63: 64: 64: 67: 67] sts.
Change to 4mm (US 6) needles.
Now work in patt as folls:
Row 1 (RS): K13 [2: 10: 11: 11: 5: 5: 13: 13], ★ place marker on needle, K2, place another marker on needle, K11, rep from ★ to last 2 [4: 12: 0: 0: 7: 7: 2: 2] sts, (place marker on needle, K2, place another marker on needle) 0 [1: 1: 0: 0: 1: 1: 0: 0] times, K2 [2: 10: 0: 0: 5: 5: 2: 2].
Markers identify '2 ladder stitches'.
Row 2: P13 [2: 10: 11: 11: 5: 5: 13: 13], ★ slip marker onto right needle, P2, slip marker onto right needle, P11, rep from ★ to last 2 [4: 12: 0: 0: 7: 7: 2: 2] sts, (slip marker onto right needle, P2, slip marker onto right needle) 0 [1: 1: 0: 0: 1: 1: 0: 0] times, P2 [2: 10: 0: 0: 5: 5: 2: 2].
These 2 rows form patt, slipping markers on every row.
Cont in patt, shaping sides by inc 1 st at each end of 9th [9th: 9th: 9th: 7th: 5th: 5th: 5th: 3rd] and every foll 12th [12th: 12th: 12th: 8th: 8th: 6th: 6th: 4th] row to 62 [64: 67: 79: 79: 88: 82: 93: 75] sts, then on every foll 14th [14th: 14th: -: 10th: -: 8th: 8th: 6th] row until there are 68 [72: 75: -: 85: -: 92: 97: 101] sts, taking inc sts into patt.
Cont straight until sleeve meas 43 [44: 44: 45: 45: 45: 45: 45: 45] cm, ending with RS facing for next row.
Shape raglan
When working shaping you will need to make ladder sts as explained in the special abbreviation section. When casting off over the 'ladder stitches' do so as folls:
Sizes 71-76, 81-86 and 112-117cm only
Cast off 5 [5: -: -: 6: -: -: -: -] sts at beg of next 2 rows. 58 [62: -: -: 73: -: -: -: -] sts.
Sizes 91-97, 102-107, 122-127, 132-137, 142-v147 and 152-157cm only
Next row: Cast off - [-: 3: 5: -: 3: 5: 1: 3] sts (one st on right needle), remove marker, 'make a ladder st', cast off - [-: 1: 0: -: 3: 2: 6: 4] sts, patt to last - [-: 6: 8: -: 6: 8: 4: 6] sts, remove marker, 'make a ladder st', remove marker, K - [-: 4: 6: -: 4: 6: 2: 4].
Next row: Cast off - [-: 4: 5: -: 6: 7: 7: 7] sts, patt to end. - [-: 65: 67: -: 74: 76: 81: 85] sts.
All sizes
(**Note:** When losing a stitch between markers due to working the ladder at the raglan shaping, do not decrease for the raglan on that row. Instead work K3 at raglan edges of the RS row. Stitch counts are not given after each row when decreases are made. Please refer to the stitch count after shaping is complete for the final figure.)

Working all raglan decreases in same way as back raglan armhole decreases, dec 1 st at each end of next and 5 [4: 5: 6: 4: 7: 8: 6: 6] foll 4th rows, then on foll 12 [15: 16: 16: 21: 18: 18: 23: 25] alt rows.
22 [22: 21: 21: 21: 22: 22: 21: 21] sts.
Work 1 row, ending with RS facing for next row.
Cast off rem sts, working ladders on rem ladder sts.

MAKING UP
Press as described on the information page.
Join raglan seams using back stitch, or mattress stitch if preferred.

Front band
With RS facing and using 3¼mm (US 3) circular needle and beg and ending at front cast-on edges, pick up and knit 82 [85: 88: 90: 90: 91: 91: 94: 94] sts up right front opening edge to beg of front slope shaping, 64 [67: 69: 72: 76: 79: 81: 83: 87] sts up right front slope, and 21 [21: 20: 20: 20: 21: 21: 20: 20] sts across right sleeve top, 26 [26: 26: 28: 28: 30: 30: 30: 30] sts from back neck, then pick up and knit 21 [21: 20: 20: 20: 21: 21: 20: 20] sts across left sleeve top, 64 [67: 69: 72: 76: 79: 81: 83: 87] sts down left front slope to beg of front slope shaping, and 82 [85: 88: 90: 90: 91: 91: 94: 94] sts down left front opening edge. 360 [372: 380: 392: 400: 412: 416: 424: 432] sts.
Row 1 (WS): K1, P2, ★K2, P2, rep from ★ to last st, K1.
Row 2: K3, ★P2, K2, rep from ★ to last st, K1.
These 2 rows form rib.
Cont in rib for a further 25 rows, ending with RS facing for next row.
Cast off in rib.

Belt
Using 3¼mm (US 3) needles and cast on 16 sts.
Beg with row 2, cont in rib as given for front band until belt meas 150 [160: 170: 180: 190: 200: 210: 220: 230] cm, ending with RS facing for next row.
Cast off in rib.
See information page for finishing instructions, threading belt through back waist casing.

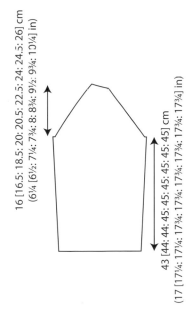

16 [16.5: 18.5: 20: 20.5: 22.5: 24: 24.5: 26] cm
(6¼ [6½: 7¼: 7¾: 8: 8¾: 9½: 9¾: 10¼] in)

43 [44: 44: 45: 45: 45: 45: 45: 45] cm
(17 [17¼: 17¼: 17¾: 17¾: 17¾: 17¾: 17¾: 17¾] in)

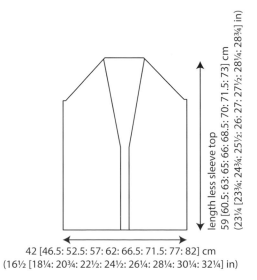

59 [60.5: 63: 65: 66: 68.5: 70: 71.5: 73] cm
(23¼ [23¾: 24¾: 25½: 26: 27: 27½: 28¼: 28¾] in)
length less sleeve top

42 [46.5: 52.5: 57: 62: 66.5: 71.5: 77: 82] cm
(16½ [18¼: 20¾: 22½: 24½: 26¼: 28¼: 30¼: 32¼] in)

Information

TENSION

Obtaining the correct tension is perhaps the single factor which can make the difference between a successful garment and a disastrous one. It controls both the shape and size of an article, so any variation, however slight, can distort the finished garment. Different designers feature in our books and it is their tension, given at the start of each pattern, which you must match. We recommend that you knit a square in pattern and/ or stocking stitch (depending on the pattern instructions) of perhaps 5 - 10 more stitches and 5 - 10 more rows than those given in the tension note. Mark out the central 10cm square with pins. If you have too many stitches to 10cm try again using thicker needles, if you have too few stitches to 10cm try again using finer needles. Once you have achieved the correct tension your garment will be knitted to the measurements indicated in the size diagram shown at the end of the pattern.

CHART NOTE

Many of the patterns in the book are worked from charts. Each square on a chart represents a stitch and each line of squares a row of knitting. Each colour used is given a different letter and these are shown in the materials section, or in the key alongside the chart of each pattern. When working from the charts, read odd rows (K) from right to left and even rows (P) from left to right, unless otherwise stated. When working lace from a chart it is important to note that all but the largest size may have to alter the first and last few stitches in order not to lose or gain stitches over the row.

WORKING A LACE PATTERN

When working a lace pattern it is important to remember that if you are unable to work both the increase and corresponding decrease and vice versa, the stitches should be worked in stocking stitch.

KNITTING WITH COLOUR

There are two main methods of working colour into a knitted fabric: **Intarsia** and **Fairisle** techniques. The first method produces a single thickness of fabric and is usually used where a colour is only required in a particular area of a row and does not form a repeating pattern across the row, as in the fairisle technique.

Fairisle type knitting: When two or three colours are worked repeatedly across a row, strand the yarn not in use loosely behind the stitches being worked. If you are working with more than two colours, treat the "floating" yarns as if they were one yarn and always spread the stitches to their correct width to keep them elastic. It is advisable not to carry the stranded or "floating" yarns over more than three stitches at a time, but to weave them under and over the colour you are working. The "floating" yarns are therefore caught at the back of the work.

Intarsia: The simplest way to do this is to cut short lengths of yarn for each motif or block of colour used in a row. Then joining in the various colours at the appropriate point on the row, link one colour to the next by twisting them around each other where they meet on the wrong side to avoid gaps. All ends can then either be darned along the colour join lines, as each motif is completed or then can be "knitted-in" to the fabric of the knitting as each colour is worked into the pattern. This is done in much the same way as "weaving- in" yarns when working the Fairisle technique and does save time darning-in ends. It is essential that the tension is noted for intarsia as this may vary from the stocking stitch if both are used in the same pattern.

FINISHING INSTRUCTIONS

After working for hours knitting a garment, it seems a great pity that many garments are spoiled because such little care is taken in the pressing and finishing process. Follow the text below for a truly professional-looking garment.

PRESSING

Block out each piece of knitting and following the instructions on the ball band press the garment pieces, omitting the ribs. Tip: Take special care to press the edges, as this will make sewing up both easier and neater. If the ball band indicates that the fabric is not to be pressed, then covering the blocked out fabric with a damp white cotton cloth and leaving it to stand will have the desired effect. Darn in all ends neatly along the selvedge edge or a colour join, as appropriate.

STITCHING

When stitching the pieces together, remember to match areas of colour and texture very carefully where they meet. Use a seam stitch such as mattress stitch or back stitch for all main knitting seams and join all ribs and neckband with mattress stitch, unless otherwise stated.

CONSTRUCTION

Having completed the pattern instructions, join left shoulder and neckband seams as detailed above. Sew the top of the sleeve to the body of the garment using the method detailed in the pattern, referring to the appropriate guide:

Straight cast-off sleeves: Place centre of cast-off edge of sleeve to shoulder seam. Sew top of sleeve to body, using markers as guidelines where applicable.

Square set-in sleeves: Place centre of cast-off edge of sleeve to shoulder seam. Set sleeve head into armhole, the straight sides at top of sleeve to form a neat right-angle to cast-off sts at armhole on back and front.

Shallow set-in sleeves: Place centre of cast off edge of sleeve to shoulder seam. Match decreases at beg of armhole shaping to decreases at top of sleeve. Sew sleeve head into armhole, easing in shapings.

Set-in sleeves: Place centre of cast-off edge of sleeve to shoulder seam. Set in sleeve, easing sleeve head into armhole.

Join side and sleeve seams.
Slip stitch pocket edgings and linings into place.
Sew on buttons to correspond with buttonholes.
Ribbed welts and neckbands and any areas of garter stitch should not be pressed.
Wash as directed on the ball band.

ABBREVIATIONS

K	knit
P	purl
st(s)	stitch(es)
inc	increas(e)(ing)
dec	decreas(e)(ing)
st st	stocking stitch (1 row K, 1 row P)
g st	garter stitch (K every row)
beg	begin(ning)
foll	following
rem	remain(ing)
rev st st	reverse stocking stitch (1 row K , 1 row P)
rep	repeat
alt	alternate
cont	continue
patt	pattern
tog	together
mm	millimetres
cm	centimetres
in(s)	inch(es)
RS	right side
WS	wrong side
sl 1	slip one stitch
psso	pass slipped stitch over
p2sso	pass 2 slipped stitches over
tbl	through back of loop
M1	make one stitch by picking up horizontal loop before next stitch and knitting into back of it
M1P	make one stitch by picking up horizontal loop before next stitch and purling into back of it
yfwd	yarn forward
yrn	yarn round needle
meas	measures
0	no stitches, times or rows
-	no stitches, times or rows for that size
yon	yarn over needle
yfrn	yarn forward round needle
wyib	with yarn at back
wyif	with yarn at front

CROCHET TERMS

UK crochet terms and abbreviations have been used throughout. The list below gives the US equivalent where they vary.

ABBREVIATIONS

UK (US)

dc (sc)	double crochet (single crochet)
htr (hdc)	half treble (half double crochet)
tr (dc)	treble (double crochet)
dtr (tr)	double treble (treble)

EXPERIENCE RATING

(Guidance only)

● ○ ○ ○ Beginner Techniques

For the beginner knitter, basic garment shaping and straight forward stitch technique.

● ● ○ ○ Simple Techniques

Simple straight forward knitting, introducing various shaping techniques and garments.

● ● ● ○ Experienced Techniques

For the more experienced knitter, using more advanced shaping techniques at the same time as colourwork or different stitch techniques.

● ● ● ● Advanced Techniques

Advanced techniques used, using advanced stitches and garment shapings and more challenging techniques

Bedecked Haberdashery
The Coach House
Barningham Park
Richmond
DL11 7DW
www.bedecked.co.uk
01833 621 451
Judith.lewis@bedecked.co.uk

Fitting

When you knit and wear a Rowan design we want you to look and feel fabulous. This all starts with the size and fit of the design you choose. We have recently increased our size range to help you achieve the best fit for your knitwear. Our womenswear sizes range from 28" (71cm) through to 62" (147cm) chest. Whilst our menswear and unisex sizes range from 32" (81cm) to 62" (152cm).

Dimensions in the charts below are body measurements, not garment dimensions, therefore please refer to the measuring guide to help you to determine which is the best size for you to knit.

STANDARD SIZING GUIDE FOR WOMEN

The sizing within this chart is based on the larger measurements within the range.

To fit bust	28 – 30	32 – 34	36 – 38	40 – 42	44 – 46	48 – 50	52 – 54	56 – 58	60 – 62	inches
	71 – 76	81 – 86	91 - 97	102 – 107	112 – 117	122 – 127	132 – 137	142 – 147	142 – 147	cm
To fit waist	20 – 22	24 – 26	28 – 30	32 – 34	36 – 38	40 – 42	44 – 46	48 – 50	48 – 50	inches
	51 – 56	61 – 66	71 – 76	81 – 86	91 – 97	102 – 107	112 – 117	122 – 127	122 – 127	cm
To fit hips	30 – 32	34 – 36	38 – 40	42 – 44	46 – 48	50 – 52	54 – 56	58 – 60	58 – 60	inches
	76 – 81	86 – 91	97 – 102	107 – 112	117 – 122	127 – 132	137 – 142	147 – 152	147 – 157	cm

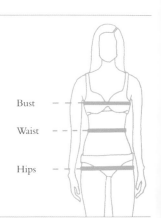

Bust
Waist
Hips

STANDARD MENS AND UNISEX SIZING GUIDE

The sizing within this chart is based on the larger measurements within the range.

To fit Chest	32-34	36-38	40-42	44-46	48-50	52-54	56-58	52-54	60-62	inches
	81-86	91-97	102-107	112-117	122-127	132-137	142-147	132-137	152-157	cm
To fit waist	24-26	28-30	32-34	36-38	40-42	44-46	48-50	44-46	52-54	inches
	61-66	71-76	81-86	91-97	102-107	112-117	122-127	112-117	132-137	cm

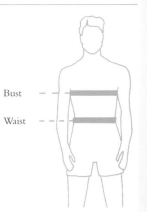

Bust
Waist

SIZING DIAGRAM NOTE

The instructions are given for the smallest size. Where they vary, work the figures in brackets for the larger sizes. One set of figures refers to all sizes.

Included with most patterns is a size diagram, see image opposite of the finished garment and its dimensions. The measurement shown at the bottom of each size diagram shows the garment width. The size diagram will also indicate how the garment is constructed, for example if the garment has a drop shoulder, this will be reflected in the drawing.

To help you choose the size of garment to knit please refer to the sizing guide. Generally in the majority of designs the welt width (at the cast on edge of the garment) is the same width as the chest.

If you don't want to measure yourself, note the size of a similar shaped garment that you own and compare it with the size diagram given at the end of the pattern.

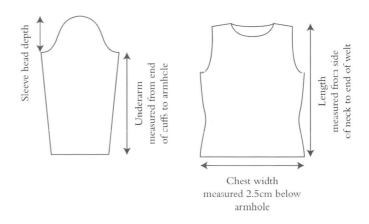

Sleeve head depth

Underarm measured from end of cuffs to armhole

Length measured from side of neck to end of welt

Chest width measured 2.5cm below armhole

MEASURING GUIDE

For maximum comfort and to ensure the correct fit when choosing a size to knit, please follow the tips below when checking your size. Measure yourself close to your body, over your underwear and don't pull the tape measure too tight!

Bust/chest | measure around the fullest part of the bust/chest and across the shoulder blades.

Waist | measure around the natural waistline, just above the hip bone.

Hips | measure around the fullest part of the bottom.

Finally, once you have decided which size is best for you, please ensure that you achieve the tension required for the design you wish to knit.

Remember if your tension is too loose, your garment will be bigger than the pattern size and you may use more yarn. If your tension is too tight, your garment could be smaller than the pattern size and you will have yarn left over.

Furthermore if your tension is incorrect, the handle of your fabric will be too stiff or floppy and will not fit properly. It really does make sense to check your tension before starting every project.

Credits

Photography | Moy Williams

Art Direction & Styling | Lisa Richardson

Model | Hattie Sewell (Boss Models)

Hair & Make Up | Michaela Taylor

Location | Peak District

Special thank you to our handknitters

Wendy Stevens | Violet Ellis | Ann Banks | Janet Oakey
Wendy Martindale | Brenda Willows | Janet Taplin

First published in Great Britain in 2021 by
Rowan
Flanshaw Lane, Alverthorpe, Wakefield,
WF2 9ND, United Kingdom
e-Mail: mail@knitrowan.com

British Library Cataloguing in Publication Data
Rowan Yarns.
Felted Tweed Collection
5010484131898
© Rowan 2021

Reprographics by Gemini Marketing Solution Ltd

Distributors

AUSTRALIA: Morris and Sons
Level 1, 234 Collins Street, Melbourne Vic 3000
Tel: 03 9654 0888 **Web**: morrisandsons.com.au

AUSTRALIA: Morris and Sons
50 York Street, Sydney NSW 2000
Tel: 02 92998588 **Web**: morrisandsons.com.au

AUSTRIA: DMC
5 Avenue de Suisse BP 189, Illzach (France)
Email: info-FR@dmc.com

BELGIUM: DMC
5 Avenue de Suisse BP 189, Illzach (France)
Email: info-FR@dmc.com

CANADA: Sirdar USA Inc.
406 20th Street SE, Hickory, North Carolina, USA 28602
Tel: 828 404 3705 **Email**: sirdarusa@sirdar.co.uk

CHINA: Commercial Agent Mr Victor Li,
Email: victor.li@mezcrafts.com

CHINA: Shanghai Yujun CO.LTD.
*Room 701 Wangjiao Plaza, No.175 Yan'an Road, 200002
Shanghai, China*
Tel: +86 2163739785 **Email**: jessechang@vip.163.com

DENMARK: Carl J. Permin A/S
Egegaardsvej 28 DK-2610 Rødovre
Tel: (45) 36 36 89 89 **Email**: permin@permin.dk
Web: www.permin.dk

ESTONIA: Mez Crafts Estonia OÜ
Helgi tee 2, Peetri alevik, Tallinn, 75312 Harjumaa
Tel: +372 6 306 759 Email: info.ee@mezcrafts.com
Web: www.mezcrafts.ee

FINLAND: Prym Consumer Finland Oy
Huhtimontie 6, 04200 KERAVA
Tel: +358 9 274871 **Email**: sales.fi@prym.com

FRANCE: DMC
5 Avenue de Suisse BP 189, Illzach (France)
Email: info-FR@dmc.com

GERMANY: DMC
5 Avenue de Suisse BP 189, Illzach (France)
Email: info-DE@dmc.com

HOLLAND: G. Brouwer & Zn B.V.
Oudhuijzerweg 69, 3648 AB Wilnis
Tel: 0031 (0) 297-281 557 **Email**: info@gbrouwer.nl

HONG KONG: CHEER WOOL
*Unit C, 9/F, V GA Building, 532 Castle Peak Road,
Cheung Shanwan, kowloon*
Tel: 2527-3919 **Email**: *info@cheerwool.com*
Web: *www.cheerwool.com*

ICELAND: Carl J. Permin A/S
Egegaardsvej 28, DK-2610 Rødovre
Tel: (45) 36 72 12 00 **Email**: permin@permin.dk
Web: www.permin.dk

ITALY: DMC
Via Magenta 77/5, Rho (Milano)
Email: info-IT@dmc.com

JAPAN: DMC KK
*Santo Building 7F,13, Kanda Konya Cho, Chiyodaku,
101-0035 , Tokyo*
Email: ouchi@dmc-kk.com

KOREA: My Knit Studio
3F, 59 Insadong-gil, Jongno-gu, 03145, Seoul
Tel: 82-2-722-0006 **Email**: myknit@myknit.com
Web: www.myknit.com

LATVIA: Latvian Crafts
12-2, Jurġu street, LV-2011
Tel: +371 37 126326825
Email: vjelkins@latviancrafts.lv
Web: www.latviancrafts.lv

LEBANON: y.knot
Saifi Village, Mkhalissiya Street 162, Beirut
Tel: (961) 1 992211 **Email**: y.knot@cyberia.net.lb

LITHUANIA: UAB GERAS KRAITIS
Jonavos 68F, Kaunas, Kaunas, LT-44191
Tel: 37067153080 **Email**: *info@geraskraitis.lt*

LUXEMBOURG: DMC
5 Avenue de Suisse BP 189, Illzach (France)
Email: info-FR@dmc.com

NEW ZEALAND: Trendy Trims
Onehunga, Auckland, New Zealand
Email: trendy@trendytrims.co.nz
Web: trendytrims.co.nz

NORWAY: Carl J. Permin A/S
Andersrudveien 1, 1914, Ytre Enebakk
Tel: 23 16 35 30 **Email**: permin@permin.dk
Web: www.permin.dk

PORTUGAL: DMC
*P. Ferrocarriles Catalanes, 117 oficina 34, Cornellá de
llobregat, 08940*
Email: info-PT @dmc.com

RUSSIA: Family Hobby
Zelenograd, Haus 1505, Raum III, 124683
Email: tv@fhobby.ru **Web**: www.family-hobby.ru

SOUTH AFRICA: Arthur Bales LTD
62 4th Avenue, Linden 2195
Tel: (27) 11 888 2401 **Email**: info@arthurbales.co.za
Web: www.arthurbalcs.co.za

SPAIN: DMC
*P. Ferrocarriles Catalanes, 117 oficina 34, Cornellá de
llobregat, 08940*
Email: info-SP @dmc.com

SWEDEN: Carl J. Permin A/S
Skaraborgsvägen 35C, 3tr, Borås
Tel: 33 12 77 10 **Email**: sverige@permin.dk
Web: www.permin.dk

SWITZERLAND: DMC
5 Avenue de Suisse BP 189, Illzach (France)
Email: info-DE@dmc.com

UKRAINE: Premium Yarn
406 20th Mishugi str, 10 #216, Kiev
Tel: +380503101008
Email: premiumyarn.ua@gmail.com
Web: www.premiumyarn.com.ua

U.S.A.: Sirdar USA Inc
406 20th Street SE, Hickory, North Carolina, USA 28602
Tel: 828 404 3705 **Email**: sirdarusa@sirdar.co.uk
Web: www.sirdar.com

U.K: Rowan
*Flanshaw Lane, Alverthorpe, Wakefield, WF2 9ND,
United Kingdom*
Tel: 01924 371501 **Email**: mail@knitrowan.com

For more stockists in all countries please logon to
www.knitrowan.com